A PHILOSOPHY OF TEXTILE

A PHILOSOPHY OF TEXTILE

Between Practice and Theory

CATHERINE DORMOR

BLOOMSBURY VISUAL ARTS
LONDON · NEW YORK · OXFORD · NEW DELHI · SYDNEY

BLOOMSBURY VISUAL ARTS
Bloomsbury Publishing Plc
50 Bedford Square, London, WC1B 3DP, UK
1385 Broadway, New York, NY 10018, USA

BLOOMSBURY, BLOOMSBURY VISUAL ARTS and the Diana logo are trademarks of
Bloomsbury Publishing Plc

First published in Great Britain 2020

Copyright © Catherine Dormor, 2020

Catherine Dormor has asserted her right under the Copyright, Designs and Patents Act,
1988, to be identified as Author of this work.

For legal purposes the Acknowledgements on p. ix constitute an extension
of this copyright page.

Cover design by Sam Clark
Cover image: *Shimmer* (2009), digital print on silk. © Catherine Dormor

All rights reserved. No part of this publication may be reproduced or transmitted
in any form or by any means, electronic or mechanical, including photocopying,
recording, or any information storage or retrieval system, without prior
permission in writing from the publishers.

Bloomsbury Publishing Plc does not have any control over, or responsibility for, any
third-party websites referred to or in this book. All internet addresses given in this
book were correct at the time of going to press. The author and publisher regret any
inconvenience caused if addresses have changed or sites have ceased to exist,
but can accept no responsibility for any such changes.

A catalogue record for this book is available from the British Library.

Library of Congress Cataloging-in-Publication Data
Names: Dormor, Catherine, author.
Title: A philosophy of textile: between practice and theory / Catherine Dormor.
Description: London; New York: Bloomsbury, 2020. | Includes bibliographical references.
Identifiers: LCCN 2019037341 (print) | LCCN 2019037342 (ebook) |
ISBN 9781472525659 (hb) | ISBN 9781472587268 (pb) | ISBN 9781472587251 (epub) |
ISBN 9781472587268 (ePDF)
Subjects: LCSH: Textile fabrics–Philosophy.
Classification: LCC NK8804 .D67 2020 (print) | LCC NK8804 (ebook) | DDC 746–dc23
LC record available at https://lccn.loc.gov/2019037341
LC ebook record available at https://lccn.loc.gov/2019037342

ISBN: HB: 978-1-4725-2565-9
ePDF: 978-1-4725-8726-8
eBook: 978-1-4725-8725-1

Typeset by Deanta Global Publishing Services, Chennai, India
Printed and bound in Great Britain

To find out more about our authors and books visit www.bloomsbury.com
and sign up for our newsletters.

CONTENTS

List of Plates vii
Acknowledgements ix

Introduction 1
  Textile as making: *techne* between practice and theory 4
  Weaving the chapters 5
  (Inter)mingling 8

1 Folding 11
  An unfolding of making 12
  Metaphorics and metonymy as enfolding modes for thinking 17
  Textile-space 20
  La Maison Baroque 22

2 Textile as shimmering surface 25
  Veils: A space of scintillation 28
  Faintly gleaming 29
  Illicit encounters 31
  Absurdity 34
  Through the looking glass 36

3 Seaming 41
  Seaming as Passage 44
  Hand and machine stitching 47
  Seaming as suturing 50
  Seaming as Trace 57
  Conjunctions and crossings 62

4 Textile as viscous substance 65
  Attacking the boundary 69
  Collapsing boundaries 71
  Flow 73
  Ontological secretions 75
  A substance between two states 78

5 **Fraying** 81
Frayed and fraying: A politics of translation 83
Frayed and fraying cloth: Broken and contingent 85
To the edge: Pointing away from the centre 90
Worn through 92
Fraying 96

6 **Textile as caressing subject/object** 99
Affective touching 100
Proximity 101
Opening out – becoming . . . 103
Measuring distance 106
First actions of hands 107
Synoptic–synthaesthetic caressing 109

Conclusion 111
Thinking-through-practice 111
Textile practices as methodology 112
Practice–theory interplay 114

Notes 117
Bibliography 119
Index 126

PLATES

Cover Image: *Shimmer* (2009). Digital print on silk

1. Jane Lackey, *Enveloping Space: Walk, Trace, Think*, 2014. Site-specific installation, spector ripps project space, Center for Contemporary Art, Santa Fe, New Mexico, 1,000 sq. ft
2. Jane Lackey, *Enveloping Space: Walk, Trace, Think*, 2014. Threshold: nylon cord, pine, copper crimps, rubber bands, MDF board
3. Jane Lackey, *Enveloping Space: Walk, Trace, Think*, 2014. Swipe wall and enclosed writing space: wool felt, chalk powder, MDF, polyester voile fabric, poplar, paint
4. Eva Hesse, *Right After,* 1969. Drawing, Private Collection
5. Eva Hesse, *Right After*, 1969. Fibreglass, approximately: 5 × 18 × 4 ft (152.39 × 548.61 × 121.91 cm). Milwaukee Art Museum, Gift of Friends of Art. M1970.27
6. Eva Hesse, *Right After*, 1969. Fibreglass, approximately: 5 × 18 × 4 ft (152.39 × 548.61 × 121.91 cm). Milwaukee Art Museum, Gift of Friends of Art. M1970.27
7. Tricia Middleton, *Troubles with Boundaries*, 2017 (detail) mixed media, found objects, cloth. Installation dimensions variable
8. Tricia Middleton, *Troubles with Boundaries*, 2017 (detail) mixed media, found objects, cloth. Installation dimensions variable
9. Ann Hamilton, *human carriage*, 2009. Installation, The Third Mind: American Artists Contemplate Asia: 1860–1989. Solomon R. Guggenheim Museum, New York. 30 January 2009–19 April 2009
10. Ann Hamilton, *human carriage*, 2009. Installation, The Third Mind: American Artists Contemplate Asia: 1860–1989. Solomon R. Guggenheim Museum, New York. 30 January 2009–19 April 2009
11. Kirstie MacLeod, *The Red Dress* (2009–), installation, dimensions variable
12. Kirstie MacLeod, *The Red Dress* (2009–), installation, dimensions variable
13. Rosalind Wyatt, *A boy who loved to run* (2013). Stitched running vest
14. Rosalind Wyatt, *A boy who loved to run* (2013). Stitched running vest

15 Chiharu Shiota, *After the Dream* (2009)
16 Chiharu Shiota, *After the Dream* (2009)
17 Izabel Wyrwa. *Something in the Air* (2010), installation. Wire, aluminium net, synthetic materials. Property of the artist
18 Kristi Kuder, *Cold Fusion* (2016), stainless-steel mesh, acrylic rods, beads 20"w × 23"h × 20"d
19 Miriam Medrez, *Zurciendo (Mending)* (2010), installation. Cloth, black thread, scissors, needle, ruler, paper and pencil
20 Miriam Medrez, *Zurciendo (Mending)* (2010), installation. Cloth, black thread, scissors, needle, ruler, paper and pencil
21 Kari Steihaug, *After the Market* (2009), installation. Size variable, unravelled knitted wool clothes/knitted image after the painting *The Gleaners* (1857), Jean-Francois Millet
22 Kari Steihaug, *Legacies* (2006), installation. Size variable, unravelled knitted wool clothes, spools of yarn, knitted sweater. Contemporary Art Center, Cincinnati, Ohio, 2016
23 Catherine Dormor, *Warp & Waft* (2016), digital print on silk satin and silk organza. Each 120 × 240 × 30 cm
24 Catherine Dormor, *Warp & Waft 2* (2016), digital print on silk satin and silk organza. Each 120 × 240 × 30 cm
25 Stephanie Metz. Installation view, *Flesh & Bone* wool sculptures, ArtArk Gallery, San Jose, California
26 Stephanie Metz. *Amorphozoa #1.2*, wool, 15 cm × 16.5 cm × 27 cm, 2014

ACKNOWLEDGEMENTS

This book is an exploration of working with textiles as an art practice, something I have a long-held fascination for. One of my prized possessions upon leaving home for university was my sewing machine and the possibilities it held. As I work at its successors and contemplate the to and fro of needle and thread, I find myself held between thought and action, and this lies at the heart of this book.

It has been written across a number of spaces as I relocated my life: my garden studio in Cambridge, my bedroom office in Battersea and my new workroom in Camberwell. Each of these, and the places which have offered inspiration as I travelled through them, have had their impact, and I am grateful for their existence in these times of production.

There are many influencing events and people behind the text and the images here. My colleagues and mentors in the various institutions and groups that I have worked in during this gestation period have added enormously to what has emerged; each conversation has planted seeds and added criticality to this text. My students across those same institutions have been an enormously important part of the development of the thoughts and text here; working with them causes me to pause and, in this reflection, new understandings and new approaches emerge. I want to thank the readers who have critiqued and reviewed the text and helped to shape it into a stronger form. I am indebted to the artists here who have so generously shared their images and artworks with me; I appreciate this act of open generosity and hope that I honour that here in return. I have enjoyed getting to know their works in new ways through making this book.

I want to thank the many friends who have taken an interest in this book, its progress and shared with me some of the frustrations of getting it ready for publication. Sadly, some of them will not see its final form, and I set their belief in it and in me firmly within its pages. I hope that they know that their support, care and encouragement have been meaningful and productive.

Finally, but not least, I want to acknowledge my family and their forbearance, and my two wonderful daughters who are now embarking upon their own careers as strong, independent women. I am so proud of you both and thank you both dearly for the love and support you have given me as I have stitched these ideas together. To my wonderful husband, Duncan, your belief in me and this book have been a sustaining force of nature.

INTRODUCTION

Textile is an ambiguous concept. It is material, it is concept, it is language, it is metaphor. To conceive of a philosophy of textile is to conceive of this ambiguity as a guiding principle for talking and thinking about textile. This book is concerned with focusing upon this ambiguity and the multiplicity of textile in order to think more about the ways in which these modes of textile intertwine with one another. This is rich and potent ground, offering a space for focusing upon what takes place within and between textile as practice and textile as theory.

That potency will be addressed here by taking textile processes and behaviours as a means for approaching textile from within textile practice itself. Considering these separately and then together reveals the relationships that exist between them and the ways in which they are inherently and irrevocably intertwined. Writers from philosophy, textile practice and textile theory will be drawn upon alongside artists who work with textiles to tease out and illuminate ways in which textile operates as language, concept and matter simultaneously. As this book examines textile practice mostly within a fine art context, the range of artists selected have been chosen for the ways in which they articulate the above-mentioned notions of textile's materiality and thus the ways in which their practice offers points of reflection for the textile practitioner.

To think about the relationship between textile practice and theory is to think simultaneously within the materiality and expressiveness of textile as stuff and about the use of language that textile elicits. For the practitioner, then, textile could be said to be about *knowing* cloth through handling it, through making it, through making with it. This has been considered in terms of tacit knowing that operates within a realm beyond words, actions and activity. It is a way of knowing that seems to weave itself into the body directly through the hands, eyes and body. Writers and theoreticians of textile also *know* cloth: they handle it as they weave and stitch with words and thought about textile. The ground between the two, between making and writing, is rich and vital. I want to suggest that this is an interdependent and reflexive space for textile. Such an approach has informed the choice of artists and artworks considered, with these being selected for their particular relationship with materials and materiality in their work and thus the potential to influence and expand what textile practice and textile theory might speak of.

Textile is readily considered in terms of its associations with the feminine, the domestic and craft concerns. These associations can lead to its richness and plasticity becoming overlooked or hidden and its ambiguity being regarded as a point of weakness not potency. In the late 1990s, a tradition of theorizing textile in which gender, sexuality and language were foundational was established. This book draws upon this work and writers such as Pennina Barnett (1999), Victoria Mitchell (2000), Janis Jefferies (2001), Anne Hamlyn (2003) and Claire Pajaczkowska (2005, 2007) in the United Kingdom; Jenni Sorkin (2000), Nicole Archer (2004) and Elisa Auther (2009) in the United States; Kirsty Robertson (2005) in Canada; and Bojana Pejic (2007) in Serbia. More recently, Rike Frank and Grant Watson, in *Textiles: an Open Letter* (2015), question ways in which perceptions of textile have shifted to elucidate its functionality within contemporary art practices; T'ai Smith reviews textile, in *Bauhaus Weaving Theory* (2014), demonstrating ways in which weaving operated as central to theoretical enquiry at the school; Guiliana Bruno, in *Surface: Matters of Aesthetics, Materiality and Media* (2014), while not solely focused upon textile practice in the same way as Frank and Watson, and Smith, considers ways in which fabric, its surface conditions and textural formation, becomes a site of material relations; Julia Bryan-Wilson's *Fray: Art and Textile Politics* (2017), looks at ways in which textiles disrupt binaries of high/low art in favour of a flexible model for the politics of textiles, which is formed upon its ambivalence. These add to a collection of extended texts, which include Sadie Plant (1998), Alisa Auther (2009) and Jessica Hemmings (2012, 2015), all with the aim of exploring textile as a set of vital and potent practices. Jessica Hemmings, in *The Textile Reader* (2012), highlights the concern that writing in this area largely existed in the form of previously unpublished conference papers and individual articles. *The Handbook of Textile Culture* (Clark, Conroy and Jefferies 2016) offers a useful survey of contemporary textile concerns and themes, which updates some of Hemmings' criticisms. This volume builds upon these precedents and their more recent attention in its focus upon the structure and language of textile practices. Additionally, it seeks to reveal some of the ways in which specific textile processes and behaviours have the potential to act as metaphorical models for approaching textile as both practice and theory.

In unpinning, locating and mapping textile as both practice and theory, three key terms emerge which provide the framework here: the matrix, (inter) relationships and *techne*. These terms are briefly described here and will be referred to and expanded upon throughout the following chapters. This book proposes textile as a form of mediation between matter, process and concept. In these relationships practice-based and theoretical approaches could be said to become warp and weft, loom and threads, working with each other to create textile ways of knowing, which brings the raw elements together in new configurations.

INTRODUCTION

With this in mind, the notion of the *matrix* is taken firstly in terms of its use within mathematics where its form as a rectangular array of numbers, symbols or expressions allows for the study of problems in which it is the relationships between the various elements that need to be maintained. Etymologically, the word 'matrix' comes from the Latin 'womb' or 'source' (*OED*), which is a space of growth and nurture that again foregrounds the relational. In this sense the matrix has become a feminist psychoanalytical strategy which challenges phallocentric conceptualizations in favour of non-hierarchical, non-binaristic organizing structures. This line of thought draws upon the writing and art practice of Bracha Ettinger, who proposes the matrix or matrixial borderspace as a system for thinking which dares to think about a 'jointness-in-separateness' (Ettinger 2006: 84). In this, matrixial theory echoes its mathematical counterpart in that it is relationships and interrelationships that are foregrounded.

The second of the two terms, *(inter)relationship* continues this mode of thinking and addresses relational interplay with the intention of locating textile practice and theory as being in mixture with one another. To focus upon the relational interplay is to focus upon the inner productive dynamic of repeated exchange. To put this more concretely, between two lovers the caresses arouse, which returns the arousal in a reciprocal encounter. Roland Barthes writes that these lovers 'create meaning, always and everywhere, out of nothing . . . [they are] in the crucible of meaning' (Barthes 1979: 67). The bracketing of (inter) then could be said to be Barthes' crucible: between and within the layers of a relationship that is always in the process of being formed. Textile practice–theory relationships unfold through concept, process and matter. They operate here as Barthes' crucible, establishing a terrain which folds and unfolds repeatedly, creating new areas of meaning.

The third term, *techne*, is often translated as craftsmanship, craft or art. Thus, it refers to fabrication or making something material into something new through a conscious, wilful material production. *Techne* as craftsmanship in this way encompasses not only the physical action of making but also the technological knowledge needed for production. Thus, as *techne* brings together knowledge, skill and imagination at the site of materiality, so as a philosophy it offers a means for thinking through both textile as theory and textile as practice as conjoined activities.

As writers such as Roland Barthes, Victoria Mitchell and Elaine Showalter have noted, both the woven cloth and language can be considered to have a matrixial structure. The material matrix of textile is formed predominantly through weaving, seaming and folding. Once formed, the textile matrix displays a variety of different behaviours, all of which depend upon the underlying structures. Three such behaviours will be focused on here, in terms of their capacity to operate as models for thinking between textile practice and theory: textile as shimmering surface, which reflects upon ways in which textile offers a non-binary model of relationships between subject and object; textile as viscous substance, which considers textile's materiality, specifically how it functions in relation to the body across which it falls; and textile as caressing subject–object, in which the key focus is upon ways that cloth caresses the body through clothing and becomes a mode of mutual and reciprocal sharing of space.

Arising from textile practices the associated and yet differentiated processes of folding, fraying and seaming are here drawn upon as textile-based themes that allow scope for thinking through and about textile practices directly. Textile offers itself as agent for joining and combining elements through a range of activities and processes. These extend and complicate notions of juxtapositioning, collaging and abutting. By focusing upon folding (Chapter 1), seaming (Chapter 3) and fraying (Chapter 5), I want to highlight ways in which textile processes reveal the ambiguity of textile and thus allow the expansion of a philosophy of textile that traverses between practice and theory. This is to operate within Ettinger's matrixial borderspace, becoming the modes and processes by which that matrix is created.

Textile as making: *techne* between practice and theory

Roland Barthes highlights the role of *techne* within the making of the text in his unpacking of the (inter) relationships between text, tissue and truth (Barthes 1973: 64). Barthes' text will be familiar to those thinking about textile practice, and thus it can readily establish a clichéd relationship between textile and text based upon the similarity of the words. I want to think here about its potential as a mode by which to access and reveal textile and textile practices as explorations of its ambiguity and thus ways in which a philosophy of textile can be conceived. Barthes, in *The Pleasure of the Text*, is establishing a set of ideas about literary theory, specifically highlighting what he calls *plaisir* and *jouissance as* effects of text. Through asserting that '*Text* means *Tissue*', he makes an association that immediately resonates, and it is easy to glide over the rest of the passage. However, the generative and physical aspects of this metaphorical and etymological association are worth further consideration. Here Barthes draws attention to the material creation of the text and tissue, but he further suggests that through its generation the subject, the author, the weaver or the artist delivers meaning over to the reader. In this 'unmaking' hyphology, a study of the tissue, Barthes attends to intertextuality: the in-between aspects of textual construction. Nancy K. Miller suggests that Barthes' *hyphology* privileges 'the mode of production over the subject' (1986: 273), but I want to suggest that what Barthes proposes is an adverbial and ongoing mode of production that is concerned with maintaining continuity between subject and object, text and textile. Thought of in these terms, textile practice and theory are bound together in producing each other, and it is this continuity that forms a matrix of meaning.

Capitalizing and extending textile's potency as maker of meaning and also as agent for material–text interstices, this book focuses upon the interplay between practice and theory through textile's materiality. Following Barthes, material and materiality are always and simultaneously *in* the process of textile production and *within* the process of its expression, offering metaphorical and practice modes for thinking about textile that involve and engage the substance, its structure and its processes.

To develop a philosophy of textile is to think through practice or making, and it is a mode of conscious experiencing that draws on phenomenological approaches. This places a particular focus on intersubjectivity and thus allows for the location of the subject to be variable or empathic. Maurice Merleau-Ponty's phenomenological studies in particular situate such an approach as foundational to the lived experience and suggest that the 'mind [is] the *other side* of the body' (1964b: 259). A phenomenological approach enables thinking from and through a lived, concrete experiencing. It is a position which foregrounds modes of knowing derived firstly through the body and the senses. Extending the phenomenological approach of Merleau-Ponty, I will also adopt a psychoanalytical reading of textile as practice, an approach which considers the responsiveness to the phenomenological live experience. Taken together, the phenomenological and psychoanalytical offer a rich and enfolded model for approaching a philosophy of textile.

The ideas and thoughts that initiated this book were driven by the desire to consider ways in which textile can open up spaces of understanding in which the interplay between textile as practice and textile as theory can be articulated. The textile works here offer entry into these spaces through both making and thinking with textile.

Weaving the chapters

To think of folding (Chapter 1) as a foundational methodology by which to articulate a textile philosophy starts from Gilles Deleuze's *The Fold: Leibniz & the Baroque* (1988). The fold disrupts the linear and planar in favour of a labyrinthine path which necessitates doubling back on oneself, a movement which is not simply a reversal but rather a form of return. Folding is an impermanent act and thus the doubling back also implies unfolding, enfolding and re-folding. What emerges from this can be thought of as an expression of continuous movement within folds or a performance of an arabesque. In the artwork of American textile artist Jane Lackey, I want to suggest that the movement of the arabesque and the return it brings about is a way into thinking about the interplay between textile practices and thinking within the fold.

'Textile as Shimmering Surface' (Chapter 2) considers textile surfaces through the lens of Roland Barthes' concept of the Neutral. This sets textile as the active, affective agent and taken together with Cixous and Derrida's dialogue on short-sightedness, *Veils* (2001), surface and depth become reactivated. Where Barthes' Neutral hovers tremulously, short-sightedness withholds clarity in favour of ambiguity. These two modes of the shimmer offer a particular reading of textile practice in which the cloth mediates encounter. These ideas are explored through the practice of 1960s artist Eva Hesse and contemporary Canadian textile artist Tricia Middleton. Hesse's practice, which she herself termed 'absurd' (Hesse in Lippard 1992: 185), carries parallels with Barthes' Neutral in that they both resist polarization, which could be seen as an economy of loss (Fer 2009: 58), but it offers instead a place for defying logic. The play of light upon the shimmering surface promises an economy in which object and reflection are conflated and confused. In the same way Middleton's work reframes domestic space, household detritus and overconsumption as altered syntax to reposition them in a tensional field between object and image.

In 'Seaming' (Chapter 3), I want to reconsider the process and notion of making a seam and its capacity to extend the cloth. This places the status of conjunctions, crossings, edges, boundaries and exchanges as key ideas in terms of their usefulness in constructing a textile matrix. This chapter starts from Frank's *Textiles: an Open Letter* (2015), which positions textile's potency as a network. Taken together with Elaine Showalter's notion of women's writing practice as a form of patchwork quilt construction, it enables the focus to be upon the seam as the scaffold for thinking. The seam here is taken as a performative act: as suture, as trace and as passage, each act and action tracing needle and thread to and fro between the fragments of cloth. The artists Ann Hamilton and Kirstie MacLeod take up these themes, performing and seaming labour and meaning-making within their work. In so doing they foreground the production of art, or the work of art, as needle and thread, championing both structural and conceptual notions of the seam in the creation of a 'new' fabric.

To think of 'Textile as Viscous Substance' (Chapter 4) is to locate it as matter somewhere between pure liquid and pure solid. Approached through texts from John Paul Sartre and Mary Douglas, the concept of 'stickiness' offers a focal point. This stickiness becomes a way of thinking of textile and textile practice in terms of not only its ambiguity but also the ways in which it activates its ability to be language, concept and matter simultaneously. Alongside these discussions, the artwork of Rosalind Wyatt, Julie René de Cotret and Elinor Whidden, and Chiharu Shiota highlight bodily metaphors and activities associated with the viscous. This includes boundaries between interior and exterior spaces, the nature of viscous substances such as chocolate, latex and wool, and ways in which the viscosity of uncertainty and the mutability of gender can act as themes for articulating textile. Themes of fluidity and flow, interior and exterior and textile's tensional fields both metaphoric and physical come to the fore here, emphasizing textile's sticky, clinging relationship with the body and its narratives.

The notion of fraying cloth as a mode by which to reveal and release implicit and tacit knowledge from practice lies in the breaking down of cloth's structural elements: the warp and weft. In 'Fraying' (Chapter 5), this opening up and threat to the integrity of the cloth-matrix is offered through the metaphor of language and the ways in which language and meaning cross and slip between users. This is to suggest a porous space of exchange across textile practice and theory. Gayatri Spivak's explorations of the creative potential at the edges of language (1993), which draw upon Sigmund Freud's *Bahnung* or broken resistance, will be starting points for thinking in this chapter alongside both Giuliana Bruno's *Surface: Matters of Aesthetics, Materiality and Media* (2014) and Julia Bryan-Wilson's *Fray: Art and Textile Politics* (2017). Where Bruno approaches materiality in terms of material relations, thus establishing the relational interplay between structure and surface, Bryan-Wilson seeks to unravel textile practice in order to rethink or to think more flexibly about what the politics of textile can be. Both approaches speak of the ambiguity of textile and thus the ways in which its material and metaphorical malleability can become vehicles for thinking at a local, intimate level and for strategic and political ends. Frayed and fraying cloth reveals its structure, opening up a field for negotiation and conversation across the unravelling gaps, ideas that artists Izabela Wyrwa, Kirsti Swee Kuder and Miriam Medrez take up within their artworks. Where in Wyrwa's work delicate constructions fray and fragment, balancing between tangible and elusive, Kuder deconstructs woven steel mesh, the mark of its former existence forever held in the warp and weft, a memory constantly reminding. Mexican artist Medrez, by way of triangulating the discussion, is figurative and expressionistic, filled with female figures, whose own edges are frayed and broken in an echo of *l'écriture feminine* in its pieced and blocked forms. For all three their work appears to be constantly in a state of flux between their making and unmaking that could be considered to be a form of performed potentiality at its very edges – that is, their work disrupts and destabilizes the narratives from the edge. In their practice, the unravelling or fraying bring centre and edge together within the fold of the work's performativity, altering and changing at the same time as revealing their formative structures.

In the final chapter, 'Textile as caressing subject/object', there is a focus upon a feminist notion of the caress as a form of porous communication between two bodies. This caress is not premised upon sexual gratification but rather upon relational interplay, taking dermis and epidermis as sites of exchange. The caress as an intra-bodily set of acts becomes here a way of thinking about textile and its relationship to the body. This is a relationship that functions materially and physically, but also culturally and psychologically. In this sense, the textile becomes a gesture towards, and with, the skin of that body. Luce Irigaray's caress and Laura U. Marks' concept of 'haptic visuality' (1999: xi) become here useful points for departure in suggesting that a porous dermality makes possible generative and productive modes of communication. I want to suggest that this porous dermality can be thought about as a gesture space in an echo of Irigaray, in which textile, body and skin operate together, intimately and without mediation. The work of three artists are discussed within this chapter – Kari Steihaug's, Stephanie Metz's and my own – all of which highlight the female body as a site for the caress as a primal gesture between two (bodies) and with multiple origins.

(Inter)mingling

This book, in its concern for the interplay between textile practice and theory, takes as a focus the (inter)mingling which occurs between these approaches. The term (inter)mingling is drawn from the subtitle of philosopher Michel Serres' looping, leaping and pooling text, *The Five Senses: A Philosophy of Mingled Bodies* (1985). In his introduction to the English translation, Steven Connor describes the text as a maze, a necessary tactic for Serres to adopt in order to move away from the hierarchical division of the senses reaching back to Aristotle. As a means by which to approach textile practice and theory together, it suggests a philosophy of overflowing and excess but also ambiguity.

Taking a matrixial structure for the intermingling of the senses foregrounds the relationships that are built between elements. Bracha Ettinger calls this 'jointness-in-separateness' (Ettinger 2006: 84), an approach that establishes modes for ways in which textile practice and theory come together. Serres' mingling and Ettinger's 'jointness-in-separateness' suggest a set of modes for thinking about textile practice and theory together as an embodiment of identity, that is an exchange of meaning between internal and external bodies.

To take a psychoanalytical approach is to suggest that there is, in the material culture of everyday life, a particular role for textile as an embodiment of identity. Textile, as material both physically and culturally, has been shown to hold the possibility of becoming imbued with memories, and which are then utilized at transitional moments. This cloth is malleable both physically and metaphorically, while also robust enough to hold those memories in adversity. The weave structure, with warp and weft pushed down onto each other, sharing the space in reciprocal exchange, creates a matrix upon which a rich interweaving of past, present and future can reside and regenerate. Textile's material particularity and its associations with the body opens it out as a potent interpretive and expressive tool.

INTRODUCTION

Psychoanalyst Melanie Klein articulated a model of 'object relations', primitive defences through which the infant combats the anxieties threatening to overwhelm. In a development of this, paediatrician and psychoanalyst Donald Winnicott suggested that certain objects, 'transitional objects', can operate as mediating tissue between the infant and the external world at this point of recognition of separateness from the m(other) (Winnicott 1953: 89). Claire Pajaczkowska (in Bryant and Pollock 2010: 134–49) offers a further development of this model, drawing upon Peircean[1] notions of the sign to consider textile as virtual and signifier. Similarly, Jenni Sorkin in her essay 'Stain: on cloth, stigma and shame' (2000) reflects upon the notion of stained cloth as a cultural signifier that disrupts normality and consistency. Textile objects are, as a result of both proximity and intimate relationship with the body, readily taken up for this role.

Taken collectively, these texts support Winnicott's illustration of his theory primarily with textile objects. They are not incidental; there is the suggestion that focusing upon textile, together with its physical, proximal and cultural materiality, opens up a space for considering its ability to affect changes in object/subject relations that corresponds to formative and transitory aspects of the formation of identity. If, as Roland Barthes suggests, text is made generatively 'in a perpetual interweaving' (Barthes 1973: 64) and, as Sorkin asserts, the stained cloth results in 'an always present-past for the wearer' (79), then setting textile as an exemplar for the transitional object is to foreground its potency as a model for the intermingling between practice and theory.

Pamela Johnson, in her text *Ideas in the Making* (1998), refers to the practice of the artist-research as 'theory in practice/practice in theory' (13), thus questioning whether this interplay is a place of productivity or constraint and placing tacit and yet powerful meaning upon the *solidus* (/). Commonly used in English as a substitute for 'or', the *solidus* indicates alternative words or perspectives and as such signifies that there is something happening within the gap or space between the elements. Thus, while suggesting the notion of choice (often mutually exclusive), Johnson suggests that the *solidus* juxtaposes and draws attention to similarities at the same time as differences. Hence, the questions she raises regarding the relationship between theory and practice sets up a dynamic of each towards the other, the *solidus* offering a nuancing of that discussion by signalling these associations towards each other. Thus the *solidus* offers scope for theoretical perspectives to inform practice-based thinking and making at the same time as practice-based thinking informs the theoretical, setting the processes of both writing and making as formative and generative activities operating together.

One of the driving forces behind this book has been to consider ways in which hands and eyes, processes and structures, practice and theory come together at and on the surface of the cloth. Thus, the materiality, the matter-li-ness, of that cloth takes centre stage here as a means by which to consider models for these relationships from within the processes of textile production and textile behaviour.

Having said that, the aim here is not to develop philosophies *about* the production of cloth nor *about* cloth's behaviours, but rather about the potential for these aspects of cloth to be drawn upon to focus upon ways in which textile is both practice and theory. This brings Johnson's *solidus* back into focus as setting intertwined and interdependent relationship between practice and theory. In developing these ideas, theoretical perspectives and precedents which draw upon woven cloth as a model will be considered in order to test their ability to act in this way. The reference here is to Gilles Deleuze and Félix Guattari's striated/smooth space and Maurice Merleau-Ponty's 'closely woven fabric' (1945: x). Whereas these establish the warp and weft within the structuring of cloth as separable and, to some extent independent, elements or binaries, the approach here will draw upon feminist thinking that places the focus more firmly on proximal affectivity and relational interplay, most particularly looking to Luce Irigaray, Bracha Ettinger and Elizabeth Grosz. In this subversion of binaristic thinking, I am proposing a mingling of textile practice and theory that 'pulsates, dances, trembles, vibrates, scintillates like a curtain of flames' (Serres 1997: 165).

1
FOLDING

According to the dictionary, to fold is to bend something such as paper or cloth so that one part of it lies on the other part. A fold is also the fenced area on a farm where sheep are kept during the night; -fold as a suffix acts as a multiplier as in threefold (*OED*). Folding bends towards, encloses and multiplies at the same time and as such can be thought of as an ambiguous activity of secretion and revelation, excess and restraint. As a structure and an action, folding resists occupying a singular space, preferring a space that has the capacity to stretch, fold and inflect. Folding establishes a new dimension upon the cartesian surface – a dimension based on form and excess. If the potency of the fold lies in the interplay between formation and its undoing, folding is inextricably caught up with unfolding. The temporary bend in the cloth relies on its opening out, its movement, to reveal itself and that which has been caught up in the fold. In many ways it is unfolding that announces the presence of folding.

When momentous events take place, analyses of the situation most commonly begin with the words 'as events unfold . . .' The phrase is used in an attempt to express the beginnings of a linear narrative, to organize and set out the stages that led to, and follow from, this current situation. However, the term unfolding reveals the complexity of events and hints at a more processual situation within which elements become uncovered, hidden and recovered by parts, not necessarily in any chronological or logical order. Events unfolding establish a map of what took place rather than a singular, linear narrative, thus implicating broader temporal events within. The fold and unfolding of events create a simultaneity of differential elements and integration.

Such events occur within a complex system in which previous events and new factors could be said to collide. The architect Bernard Tschumi states that 'an event is a kind of accident, one that arises from the unlikely collision of generally uncoordinated vectors' (Virilio and Rose 2000: xi). Thought of in this way, it makes sense then that the presence of an event is usually felt through its aftereffects.

To think of folding from the viewpoint of folded or pleated fabric focuses upon the interplay of folding and unfolding as a multiple and complex space. While the seemingly flat fabric hangs somewhat austerely from the hips, the slightest movement of the body causes those pleats to unfold and reveal their excess fabric secreted within but also the curvature of the hips, the waist and the legs that are implicated in the movement. In their unfolding, the pleats reveal their formation, in their formation their unfolding is created. This is the temporal field of the fold. It holds within itself an unfolding event: folds within folds.

An unfolding of making

In *The Fold* (1988) Gilles Deleuze takes the idea of temporality and multiple fields in considering the materiality and concept of folding and unfolding through an analysis of the role of the Baroque within the work of the mathematician Leibniz. Here he proposes the Baroque to be both identified by the fold and productive of folds and thus sets the fold in terms of a relationship with itself. This positions it within a schema of reflexive temporality in which there is no beginning and no end.

> The Baroque refers not to an essence, but rather to an operative function, to a trait. It endlessly produces folds. It does not invent things . . . the Baroque trait twists and turns in its folds, pushing them to infinity, fold over fold, one upon the other.
> (DELEUZE 1988: 3)

In this model such reflexivity enables folds within folds – relations within relations – and the very process by which an event occurs becomes clearer and yet increasingly intricate and complex. As the wearer moves, so the pleats open and close, fold back into themselves and over each other to create a swinging, undulating pattern of movement and excess.

Deleuze sets out four elements inherent to the Baroque fold:

1. Folding is an activity of continuity rather than completion
2. The active and relational interplay between folds is vital in maintaining the integrity of the fold
3. The fold does not unify but brings elements into relationship
4. Unfolding is implicated within folding and its temporal field

(Deleuze 1988: 111)

Taken together, these four elements offer a way for thinking through, and about, relationships between textile practice and theory. It is in the encounter with the other within the space of the fold that an expression of that other is created. As one element folds onto its other self, its multiplicity and capacity become revealed. Martin Heidegger believed that artworks should always be considered in terms of the event of their creation. Here, 'origin' is understood as 'that from which and by which something is what it is and as it is' (Heidegger 1993: 143). To think of it in this way is to have in mind multiple vectors that loop forward and backward within the temporal field. As with the pleated garment at rest, Tschumi's collision and Heidegger's origin hold meaning and process within the folds of fabric, extending their temporality. Process and meaning are always present and always integral parts of the whole. This greater volume becomes animated in movement and thus completes the garment through being what it is and as it is.

To conceive of folding fabric as a way of approaching the capacity for exchange between textile practice and theory also involves thinking of folding as form of deconstruction. To deconstruct and set out the constituent parts held within each element enables meaning to be exchanged at a structural level. The fold and folding is capable of establishing multiple and altering permutations – it is a process of exchange. In folding between textile practice and theory, meaning is transferred through layering and pleating, which enables an extended sense of meaning through the temporal to-ing and fro-ing between and within the folds. This recognizes the processes of meaning-making that take place *between* words as signifiers of meaning. Such multiplicity and metamorphosing together mean that folding involves a repeated and ongoing sending out and bringing back of meaning; it is reflexive and duplicitous.

This duplicity, together with the inherent reflexivity, is what Luce Irigaray refers to, in her discussion of the production of female subjectivity, as an enfolded process involving self-touching. In this she draws upon female anatomy and the configuration of the vulva as two lips, which are themselves multiple folds.

> In order to touch himself, man needs an instrument; his hand, a woman's body, language . . . and this self-caressing requires at least a minimum of activity. As for woman, she touches herself without any need for mediation, and before there is any way to distinguish activity from passivity. Woman 'touches herself' all the time . . . her genitals are formed of two lips in continuous contact.
> (IRIGARAY 1977: 24)

Here, for the woman, the folds are constantly in contact, touching and reconfiguring, creating connections within connections. Irigaray here foregrounds female subjectivity as sticky and as a series of becomings. The fold, like expression, actualizes content, so a female subjectivity as self-folding offers a way for thinking about art-making as a form of continuation of that subjectivity. Patricia MacCormack refers to this as becoming-vulva:

> In becoming-vulva new positions open new ideas which could not have existed before – the elements are the model . . . In the fold, alterity is encountered within the self, through the other, and the other encounters the self in ways the self cannot autonomously express.
>
> (MACCORMACK 2009: 106–7)

Irigaray and MacCormack, taken together, offer non-linear models for thinking about the reality of art-making as an expression of being that echo and extend Heidegger's 'origin' and Deleuze's labyrinthine internal relationships. They propose a model for the interplay between thinking and making, between the work of art and art's works, that doubles back on itself, folding and unfolding repeatedly.

Folding, unlike cutting and seaming, is an impermanent act of doubling over that further implies in its turn unfolding, enfolding and refolding. Thought of in these terms, the relational interplay between practice and theory becomes an expression of a continual and processual movement between and within those folds: always in flux, always in the process of exchange and change. Such interplay could be said to be the performance of the baroque arabesque that occurs as one fold momentarily ends and another begins. Thus, performance at the point of inflection within and between folds becomes an expression of the continual movement to and fro and the labyrinthine pathways reveal their unfoldings, re-foldings and new foldings as the folded fabric is animated across the moving body.

Pennina Barnett, in her essay accompanying the exhibition *Textures of Memory: The Poetics of Cloth* (1999), suggests that the fold offers a way for thinking through textile practice that is built upon an elasticity for thinking practice and materializing theory. Thus, she suggests that as the fabric opens and re-folds, in its volume a blurring of the binaristic either/or framework takes place:

> The poetics of cloth are a stretching out: an invitation to leap inside the hollow of the fold, to see what happens. And to think *inside the continuity of the fold* is to think in a continuous present.
>
> (BARNETT 1999: 32)

In this she suggests a methodological mode for thinking about making that foregrounds cloth-based language and behaviours, pointing towards an undulating and folding material matrix within and upon which language is not only used metaphorically but also becomes the medium of practice. Such a framework for thinking about making is constructed through the processes of that making itself, which is an enfolded framework that, like the pleated skirt, opens and flexes.

According to Deleuze, the definition of the baroque is 'the fold into infinity' (1988: 122), going beyond itself, enlarging and distending. Thus, folds are constantly in the process of revealing themselves. '[A] fold is always folded within a fold, like the cavern in a cavern . . . the smallest element of the labyrinth, is the fold, not the point' (6). Thought of in this way, folding and unfolding can no longer be taken as opposite actions, but rather they come together generatively. As the fold is unfolded, so it reveals further folds within folds and so 'to unfold is to increase, to grow' (8). Deleuze turns to the notion of metamorphosis here suggesting that 'metamorphosis . . . pertains to more than mere change of dimension: every animal is double . . . just as the butterfly is folded into the caterpillar that will soon unfold' (9). Like Irigaray's folded vulva, Deleuze here draws out the process of folding: it allows its elements to exceed and distend beyond a change of state, beyond themselves. In this sense, the fold brings together the structures of layering, but also articulation or reflexivity so that it reveals what lies within the fold: further folds and excess volume.

Thinking of the fold as a way by which to think through the production of subjectivity, folding offers itself as a critique or challenge to models which separate interiority and exteriority. Folding foregrounds the continual and processual notion of such a production, and thus the fold is both figure and ground, process and product, continuously producing itself. The fold, then, models subjectivity as a repeated, reflexive impulse.

Such reflexivity and fluidity of the subject in turn emphasizes the fold as primarily relational. Like the event, it is a mode for thinking that has the capacity to bring together elements without either a temporal or a hierarchical structure. In confounding binaries often erected to separate interiority from exteriority, the fold focuses primarily upon the involuted, and invaginated, encounter. Such an encounter is one that rejects inside and outside as structuring paradigms in favour of a terrain which holds within itself the ability to stretch, to fold and to inflect and in this way proposes itself as an active and fluid multiplicity in which the actions and activities of making are not established either as individuals or as sets of individuated process, but rather take the form of continual pleatings that fold and open against one another to reveal their volume and excess.

The work of the American textile artist Jane Lackey is a good example to focus upon here. Her practice is borne from the interplay of different media, largely textile, sculpture, performance and drawing. She moves between macro and micro approaches: between the ways in which warp folds in and around weft and the ways the body and cloth can be choreographed together. Her installations, then, hover between diagram, origins and finished works. Tangible materials (thread, chalk, felt, cords, tape and cloth) become points of inspiration, drawing materials and articulation of that practice. As the woven cloth relies on warp and weft being held together for its existence, so Lackey's practice requires all of its elements, its macro and micro concerns, to be held together: diagram, articulation, installation and points of origin fold and unfold around one another.

The notion of connectivity through repeated foldings and pleatings within foldings and pleatings suggests that otherness, or alterity, is generated within the self and revealed through the other as an enfolding and unfolding process of the creation of subjectivity. As a model within Lackey's textile practice, a mode for thinking and making, folding opens up each element's otherness within the others at the same time as recognizing their differences from between and within a seemingly endless series of unfoldings or becomings. This interplay, held within the folds, means that as the one folds together with another, the two (or even three or more) do not involute or elide, but rather from within that folding together emerges a form of meaning-making that is, like the fold itself, about volume. It is labyrinthine, elastic, pliable and multiple. Further, given that folding is foregrounded upon notions of affectivity, it operates as a model for thinking across the terrain not in terms of what each element *is* in relation to the others but in terms of what this matrixial structure, in its volume, pliability and fluidity, *does*.

Enveloping Space: Walk, Trace, Think (2014) (Plate 1) offers precisely this model of thinking across its elements, moving between diagram, model and installation to reveal both the art work and the art's work. Installed in the Center for Contemporary Art, Santa Fe, New Mexico, this site-specific installation brings together a number of parts or elements. A series of small mdf blocks suspended just off the raw concrete floor of the gallery by thick nylon cords (Plate 2), which act as a screening device behind which are a series of frames painted, stitched and drawn plans or maps on *kozo* paper. Further beyond another screen, this time loose-woven scrim a shoulder-height series of felt chalkboards are installed, whose surfaces have been chalk-inscribed, erased and re-inscribed (Plate 3). Located at the centre of the work are two benches with slots for four books and pens. Each book contains an introduction and an invitation to sit and add: a commonplace book for adding to and reading from. Each element maps spatial characteristics of architecture, landscape and interior schema; each element evokes the intimacy of body systems: familiarity, imagined or remembered. The intimate and monumental, the weave and the cloth fold and unfold onto and over one another.

To think of Lackey's installation in terms of folding is to approach the experience of walking through her practice and its processes, to trace the various connections between elements and to look forward and back upon trajectories of travel through the loosely woven scrim and hanging blocks. In her artist statement, Lackey talks of the enveloping of the elements together that each become a point of origin and together form an expanding, voluminous space of shared choreography and co-production of the work. This offers an echo of Rozsika Parker's comment on the evolution of both feminism and embroidery in her updated introduction to *The Subversive Stitch* (2010: xxi), where she notes that the pattern of progress is not linear but more one of revisitation and reflection, a fluid and constantly changing landscape. What interests me here specifically, in reference to charting the foldings and unfoldings of the installation and its elements, is how Lackey's practice loops back into the history of feminist craft practices, through a feminist art practice.

Lackey's approach to her materials has an element of the transitional: the maps, drawings, notebooks, felt and chalk become stages to work and move through and to come out of and to revisit. The maps and drawings are spare and delicate imagined schemata. The long black felt surface resembles a used blackboard in its indecipherable erasure, which evoked criticism for the installation's lack of coherence from one reviewer (Landi and Landi 2014). This returns me to Rozsika Parker's preoccupation with continuities and discontinuities, which are both found here in Lackey's folded envelopment. Through the use of textile tactics and craft practices she brings together future projections and suggested documentation without defining either didactically. What she does is to lay the ground for a rapprochement between fine art and craft practices, in both theory and practice. The installation reads as both process and product, emphasizing the dimension of labour enfolded within. Visual, spatial and temporal conversations between elements, practices, labour and thinking continue to unfold, not in lines, but as uncoordinated vectors or voluminous pleats that reveal a capaciousness and excess beyond the carefully drawn and screened work.

Metaphorics and metonymy as enfolding modes for thinking

Textile, when thought of in terms of its material presence, language and affectivity, can be said to operate as concept, metaphor and matter. It is this fluidity that means it is a medium which has been widely appropriated. Here I want to capitalize on, and extend, textile's potency as maker of meaning in terms of textile practice as a mode of expression that folds itself between material presence, language and affectivity.

Material and materiality are active simultaneously *in* the process of textile production and *within* the process of its perception, offering metaphorical and practice-based methodologies involving and engaging with the textile, its structure and its production. Michel de Certeau, in *The Practice of Everyday Life* (1984), suggests that a recipe for theory can be constructed through the model of 'cut-out and turn-over' (62), a methodology familiar to textile practitioners. In this he highlights practice–theory relationships as necessarily enfolded, noting that 'the theory belongs to the procedures it deals with' (63). Similarly, Patricia

MacCormack, writing under the title 'Becoming Vulva: flesh, folds, infinity' (2009), draws together Irigarayan and Deleuzean notions of the fold, suggesting that

> Materiality emerges through signifying systems and these systems are themselves material, thus the collision is never between two but creates an involuted encounter that dissipates molecules of each as more or less intensified in regard to moments of thought and actualisation.
> (MACCORMACK 2009: 97)

In this she creates echoes of de Certeau's cut-out and turn-over model for thinking-through-making (1984: 62), seeing it as an enfolding and unfolding relationship, between materiality, material and the processes of their construction. However, in approaching this as an event in Tschumi's terms, she suggests that relationship as voluminous and continuous in its habit, emerging as it does from multiple origins.

As the pleats of the skirt fall back onto each other, pleat falls onto and into pleat, intermingling with one another and creating new shapes and movement across the body. To think of the textile falling upon textile in this way places a particular focus on the roles of language as a mode for producing meaning through the very processes of making with textile. As a result, metaphoric and metonymic language become key structuring elements, most obviously those relating to textile, textile structure and textile production. Such an approach enables language, text and practice to work together within a matrix of interactivity.

Metaphoric language, metonymy and the use of metaphors here together enable a space for the creation of a matrix for the literal and observable enfolded together with signification to derive their meaning. Such language capitalizes upon the difference between what a statement states and what it alludes to or suggests in an act of folding. It offers possibilities and potentialities of and for meaning within the folds. In this, textile language sets its usage as an event.

Metaphor and metonymy are two modes of language which, while closely related, create meaning in different ways. The metaphor draws on similarities for meaning, and it is the syntactic context that brings the selected words into use. On the other hand, metonymy is based upon contiguity of a 'word heap' (Jakobson 1956) whereby it is the particular combination of words that creates meaning. Thus, according to Jakobson, 'I work at the coalface' is a metaphor in that it references the hard grind of a miner cutting coal in order to provoke the image of someone who does all of the hard work for the benefit of the others, while 'I'm one of the suits' is metonymy in that it substitutes the clothing of a manager for the manager himself. The balancing act between these two linguistic modes is neatly summed up by Jakobson:

> An inferior choice of words is at the sacrifice of metaphor, whereas an inferior combination of words is at the sacrifice of metonymy.
> (JAKOBSON 1956: 76)

Through this idea of the metaphor, Jakobson emphasizes the way that it draws directly on the meaning of the words selected, but through its imagery it produces intensified meaning. Held within Lackey's installation, the invitation and the words added to the commonplace book become heightened moments of enfoldment, a form of momentary distilling of that interaction secreted within the fabric and drawn folds.

On the other side of Jakobson's dualism, metonymy accretes meaning as a result of particular combinations of words, and thus later words come to clarify earlier words and earlier words clarify later ones in an enfolding and unfolding mode of meaning-making. So, the expression 'the pen is mightier than the sword' relies both on the relationship between a pen and a sword as much as between what a pen produces and what a sword potentially can do, thus the meaning of the phrase moves to and fro between the words, unfolding itself in the process.

Both metaphoric and metonymic language are modes by which meaning is extended beyond the words used. They also can be thought of as pleated or folded forms of language in that they fold imagery and associative ideas together with the signifying language; meaning continues to fold and unfold. Such a mode of thinking and meaning-making is one in which the fixed relationship between signifier and signified, sign and meaning, is exchanged and the two set in a constant state of flux in relation to each other. This fluid signifier–signified relationship is an important aspect of thinking through textile, a way of thinking in which textile metaphors and metonymies operate alongside and together with one another. Thus, here, stitch, warp, seam, fold and weft become units of meaning separately and together: signifying marks and matter.

Such use of metaphor and metonymy establishes a mode for thinking-through-making that transcends and resists interpretation. Susan Sontag, in her essay 'Against Interpretation' (1966), warns that

> In most instances, interpretation amounts to the philistine refusal to leave the work of art alone. Real art has the capacity to make us nervous. By reducing the work of art to its content and then interpreting that, one tames the work of art.
>
> (SONTAG 1966: 8)

In this she highlights the dangers inherent in attempting to interpret artwork, in trying to 'translate' art into words. Further, she suggests that this lies in the reduction of that work to its content. The metaphor sidesteps that trap, establishing language in an enfolded relationship with practice, opening up a matter-language-process matrix for thinking that is always oblique, forever mobile and provisional. This matrix seeks to talk about the relational interplay within which the work exists in terms of '*how* it is what it is, even *that* it is what it is, rather than to show what it *means*' (Sontag 1966: 10 my emphases).

Through this a matrix of meaning emerges that is both structuring and generative. It offers multiple reflexivity between material, meaning and making. The matrixial relationship reveals itself as an unfolding, emergent space, or as artist–theorist Bracha Ettinger describes it:

> In the matrix a meeting occurs . . . consist[ing] neither in fusion, nor repulsion, but in a continual readjustment of distances, a continual negotiation of separateness and distance within togetherness and proximity.
>
> (ETTINGER 2006: 14)

The matrixial relationship of togetherness and separateness builds thinking-through-making as a mode which depends upon textile practice having multiple origins: fine art, craft, industrial product, concept and metaphor. In this sense then the set of practices and methodologies involved here incorporate textile techniques and processes: stitch, weave, binding, threading, alongside linguistic practices such as metaphor and metonymy.

Textile practices take place at, on and within the folding, unfolding and enfolding terrain of the cloth, which is itself, in turn, enfolded. Deleuze and Guattari describe such thinking from material as 'the consciousness or thought of the matter-flow' (1980: 454), recognizing in this the sliding and overlapping that such an approach requires.

Textile-space

The practices or strategies of writing textile and making text together create an enfolded space, which I will refer to as textile-space, for the production, analysis and reception of textile practice and theoretical perspectives. Here multiple and mutable layers enfold meaning within and between modes of practice. This textile-space of and for thinking-through-practice allows for the different facets of textile-based language and practices not only to coexist but also to become co-producers and thus form a concommitant form of practice–research – Barnett's practice of research, or 'invitation to leap inside the hollow of the fold, to see what happens. And to think *inside the continuity of the fold*' (Barnett 1999: 32) suggests a voluminous and expansive space within the fold for thinking with textile.

In a similar vein to such elasticity of textile-thinking, the research model adopted by textile artist–theorist Janis Jefferies provides further foundations for this mode of writing textile, making text. In his introductory essay to Jefferies' *Selvedge* exhibition catalogue (Maharaj in Mitchell 2000), cultural theorist Sarat

Maharaj describes Jefferies' relationship between practice and theory as a 'print out of a long-wave *think–speak–write* sequence' (7). Such a description points to the multiple ways in which Jefferies' practice draws on textile metaphorics as agency of, and for, expression. What emerges from within this (un)folding sequence is a mode of textile-thinking–speaking–making that can be thought of as an assemblage, or tissue, of practice. This 'speaks with meanings that are tactile, corporeal and conceptual' and that 'reverberate in the plurality of possibilities within' (55). Such a pleated mode of *think–speak–write* in its folding, unfolding and refolding across time, offers scope for textile knowledge and language to come together.

To talk of textile practice as a mode of thinking is not to say that the practitioner is thinking *by means* of that practice or that their thoughts are being translated or transcribed *into* the practice. Rather, it is a form of thinking that is about the dynamic exchange *between* practitioner, tools and language that become drawn up into each other. In this way the notion of thinking or thought as a kinetic, temporal and dynamic dimension is key.

As needle and thread, shuttle and weft, move forward and backward, quickly and slowly, suddenly and hesitatingly, to and fro across and between the cloth, so that kinetic mode opens up a space for focus upon the processes and behaviours of cloth.

The textile-space highlights the continuously folding and unfolding nature of practice As Joan Simon writes in relation to artist–weaver Sheila Hicks:

> Hicks' small works are neither fragments nor details of her larger pieces . . . This is not to deny that Hicks' discoveries in her small works inform her bigger, indeed biggest, works in other ways. It is not a question of proportional magnification, however, but a question of process: a finding, an accident, a shape or material . . . these may be calculated or intuitive, restlessly careless or irregularly repetitious.
>
> (SIMON IN HICKS 2006: 58)

The notion of 'restless carelessness' and 'irregularly repetitious' is a common theme among artists and will be a theme revisited in later chapters in relation to those featured. However, it also marks the characteristically frayed and porous nature of what I have termed the textile-space. To think of this space as both porous and enfolded offers a way for talking about thinking-through-textile. Michael Polanyi, in his series of lectures 'the Tacit Dimension' (1966) stated that 'we know more than we can tell' (1966: 6), referring to those parts of the practice of performing even everyday tasks that lie beyond articulation or explication. In many ways, this is similar to Sontag's challenge to interpretation, and her preference for a focus upon '*how* it is what it is' (Sontag 1966: 10). Polanyi calls this 'know-how' and his interests lay in what it means to *know*.

From within the porous and enfolding textile-space, ways to explore, discuss and articulate textile practice emerge. This is not in order to stretch out that space and reveal it as it were a pelt from the hunted prey, but rather to offer some entry points into the labyrinthine space and some mapping points to initiate new journeys. In this sense, then, Polanyi's tacit refers not to those aspects for which words are inadequate stand-ins, perhaps even imposters, rather it refers to the broader understandings of knowledge or know-how that can be expressed and understood through their affects, metaphors and processes. Such an unfolding, enfolding and folding methodology is composed of a matrix of threads and words, loops and metaphors, intersections and spaces, textures and forms, trajectories and involutions: a proliferation of loose ends.

La Maison Baroque

In Lackey's installation *Enveloping Space*, with its three-dimensional form, the viewer is drawn into an intimate relationship with herself and the work, creating spaces in which 'you can walk - explore - respond . . . the enveloping atmosphere of translucent material filters exterior awareness leading to a gestalt of writing, making, tracing and sometimes unexpected calm' (artist statement, Center for Contemporary Art, Santa Fe, 2014).

Alongside language, models and diagrams form an important part of the practice, these might involve methodological models and working drafts that seek to explore and understand how the act of practice takes and ways in which they are used within practice to test out and explore ideas and concepts. The word 'diagram' comes from the Greek *dia* (across/through) and *gramma* (something written, a letter of the alphabet, something marked out by lines, a geometrical figure, written list, register) and is generally understood to be a simplified drawing showing the appearance, structure or workings of something; a schematic representation (*OED*). Similarly, 'model' comes from the Latin *modellus,* meaning measure or standard, and is used here in its form as a simplified representation used to explain the workings of a real-world system or event. Thought of like this, then, diagrams and models create a folding, unfolding and enfolding space that aids and expands understandings of, and thinking through, concepts and interrelationships. They make the process of practice continuous: secreting meaning within and between their folds.

According to Anthony Vidler, 'a diagram is mainly an Icon, and an icon of intelligible relations in the constitution of its Object' (Vidler 1999) and as such is an 'instrument of suspended reality'. The way in which Deleuze uses the diagram draws on these ideas for its capacity to visually articulate particular relationships and functions and thus bring together spatial and linguistic modes of expression; it is a map or machine. For both Vidler and Deleuze, then, the diagram and/

or model operate as forms of abstraction from reality that serve to highlight relational and processual aspects of a practice. The diagram and model then become enfolded structures: neither one space nor many, but a space with the capacity to stretch and fold and inflect: like the pleated skirt, voluminous and compact at the same moment.

Two models/diagrams which are of particular interest here are Deleuze's *La Maison Baroque* (Deleuze 1988: 5) and Sarat Maharaj's *JJ's Text–Tale–Telling as Protein Enzyme* (Maharaj in Mitchell 2000: 9). The first appears in the first chapter of *The Fold* and offers a model of subjectivity, an allegory derived from the philosophy of Leibniz.

Deleuze's two-floor house has a ground floor with four windows and a door with steps leading up to it. The upper level narrows to a single, closed room, lined with folded drapery and with five small openings in the floor to allow flow from below. The five openings represent the five senses, the closed chamber a mind-space whose response is based on the physical body, and the floor–ceiling structure is the porous threshold between mind and body.

In the second diagram/model Maharaj seeks to express Janis Jefferies's practice–theory interrelationship, her 'think-speak-write sequences', by drawing on the structure of a protein enzyme and the way in which these proteins act as a catalyst within chemical reactions. Each enzyme has an active site into which the substrate fits exactly, and the protein enzyme then folds around it completely, maximizing the surface it has to act upon. Maharaj's diagram shows the protein about to fold and thus brings together the various and variable (but always multiple) elements of Jefferies's practice; it also demonstrates Jefferies's thinking, which is both logical and non-linear and folds around the 'active site' as an enzyme upon its substrate, dynamic and affective sites of production of meaning. To try and read either of these models too literally would be to try to impose a fixed, singular reading and thus to miss the point of such a form of expression. Like metaphoric language, Maharaj and Deleuze's diagrams 'write through' the structure, presenting a visual aid that continues to fold, refold and unfold, producing multiple meanings and understandings. The model, like the metaphor, doesn't necessarily imply chronology or hierarchy of structure in that it has multiple origins and multiple pathways. It offers on the other hand an overview and an expression of how the various parts interrelate.

The use of models and diagrams as a tool for thinking-through-making operates as Vidler's diagram: an 'instrument of suspended reality'. In this they express the folded and folding nature of practice as interrelationships and intertwinings.

Where Lackey's screened-off sections separate, they also envelop the viewer. The work operates both as expression of the architectural space and, simultaneously, as models and diagrams within the process of forming the whole installation. In this way macro and micro thinking fold onto each other in a doubling and secreting of meaning.

Folding as a methodological approach echoes or mimics concerns or interstices between and within theoretical and practice-based concerns, it is necessarily a complex picture. As the stitches cross and intertwine with each other in seaming two pieces of cloth together, so too do the modes or models of thinking: folding, seaming and fraying together with viscosity, shimmering and caressing through cloth. In this sense, they are enfolded and unfolding modes and models.

The processes of thinking and practice take the form of seaming and folding that is found within the designer's workshop as they drape upon the form, pushing and pulling the fabric around the mannequin, cutting away pieces here and adding extra sections there until the final pattern pieces can be drafted and construction begins. In this sense, thinking-through-practice: the seaming, fraying and folding is as much about the struggle to find a voice, a way to articulate textile practice, as about how those elements eventually come together. How to write textile and make text? How to fold towards each other the subjective and the processual and the outcomes (physical, metaphorical and conceptual) without containment or elision? Thus, the terms 'folding', 'fraying' and 'seaming' are drawn upon consciously and strategically, as language that emerges from textile practice, to create a material matrix that foregrounds the adverbial and journeying nature of thinking through textile. It is the intention that the matrix formed offers a map with reference points, while enabling individual readers/viewers to navigate through it by different and differing routes, from different and differing starting points. Like Maharaj's folding protein, these are catalysts for thinking to fold around.

Within this matrix the practice–text relationship is located as inseparable and indivisible. The distinctive modes of practice embedded in the centre and at the core of this thinking relate to all of the methodological modes simultaneously. When the modes interact, they necessarily interact with and affect the other, thus establishing dynamic and matrixial dialogues that are constantly folding, unfolding and refolding between and among them.

2
TEXTILE AS SHIMMERING SURFACE

To shimmer is defined as to 'shine with a tremulous or flickering light; to gleam faintly' (*OED*) and thus to think of cloth as a shimmering surface is to focus upon the play of light across its surface, and what happens when light passes through that surface. Roland Barthes in his 1978 lecture series 'The Neutral' defined the shimmer as 'that whose aspect, perhaps whose meaning, is subtly modified according to the angle of the subject's gaze' (Barthes 1978: 51). In this he shifts the focus from the movement of light upon the surface to the position of the viewer's eye in relation to that surface.

To approach textile as a shimmering surface through Barthes' Neutral is to set textile as an active and affective agent. Hélène Cixous and Jacques Derrida, in a dialogue on short-sightedness, *Veils* (2001), establish an interplay between seeing unclearly and veiled viewing. In setting the textile as both material and metaphorical pivot, this chapter aims to establish a cloth that considers the holes and threads of the woven structure alongside more solid notions. Such thinking offers a porous, ambiguous surface whose presence lies as much in its ability to transmit light as to reflect it. The scintillation that this play of light effects brings together both Barthes and Cixous/Derrida as a mode for thinking through the ambiguity of textile and thus challenging oppositional structures.

Taken in this way, the shimmer becomes a concept or model for thinking about the interplay between textile thinking and practice as an immanent passage. Derrida talks of an 'echo of light' out in front of the dazzling clarity of the full beam of light' and at the same time out in front of the veil of myopia. The shimmering textile occupies this space, an echo of light performed through the relationship of light, surface and viewer. The shimmer reflects and is reflexive; as a model for the interplay between textile theory and practice, it offers a space for ways in which they are held together in dynamic relationship.

This chapter considers the shimmering textile from three loci and through a focus upon two artists: 'Illicit encounters', in which Eva Hesse's artwork of the late 1960s is considered in terms of Barthes' Neutral, most particularly the way in which she articulates the pictorial–sculptural encounter within her work through the use of the void; 'Absurdity', in which Hesse's work is approached in terms of its apparent lack of logic and the potential for such practice to operate as a shimmering surface of the 'not-yet'; and 'Through the Looking Glass', in which the shimmer challenges reflection through the work of Canadian contemporary artist Tricia Middleton, particularly through the ways in which her work uses textile to extend and deepen spatial limitations, confusing and confounding semiotic relationships, to open out a shimmering matrixial space at the point of reflection. Both artists, in spite of the decades between their working practices, traverse medium-specific delimitations and situate the viewer on a troubling threshold that threatens as it simultaneously invites, repels as it attracts. Both artists are preoccupied with materials and materiality, in ways associated with textile practice, making them useful and interesting points of reference here. Most particularly, in drawing on the aesthetic properties of textile and cloth, they also draw out aspects of its social and cultural connotations. So, for example, in focusing upon textile's ability to evoke ideas of connectedness and relational interplay, these artists emphasize extra-aesthetic modes of meaning-making. As the looking glass both reveals and deceives, so the works considered here hover or shimmer between object and reflection, suggesting a generative, scintillating space between the two.

Lesley Millar, in her introductory essay to the catalogue for *Lost in Lace: Transparent Boundaries* (Birmingham Museum & Art Gallery 2011), draws connections between architectural dividers of space and cloth in terms of the body, establishing both as thresholds where light and matter mingle. This exhibition builds on Millar's fascination with the interplay of textile within space and her work with artists to produce site-sensitive installations and stagings of textile. In taking this analogy from woven cloth into lace, Millar emphasizes this boundary space as fragmented and fragmentary, but nonetheless present and real:

> In the holes between the threads, the contour is present and absent simultaneously, leading our gaze through one interior to another.
> (MILLAR 2011: 6)

Lace as textile becomes an ambiguous borderline whose crossing is not always known. The traveller oscillates within and between the structure. For Millar, drawing on sociologist Richard Sennett, philosopher Walter Benjamin and the Japanese architects Junya Ishagari and Arata Isozaki, this ambiguity and hovering between positions laces as fluid and energetic, 'not quite defined, never solidified, never definitely fixed' (Millar 2011: 7).

Taken as a borderline cloth whose presence and absence together define that threshold, lace allows, even encourages, visual access between spaces. Thus, it becomes a tensional field, a flickering surface. As light passes through the holes, casting shadows, so holes and threads overlap each other and the surfaces onto which the light falls, shimmering between.

Lace offers glimpses through that oscillate between presence and absence, operating as a kind of veiled mode for perceiving. What Millar establishes through both her curating of this exhibition and the catalogue essay is the idea of lace 'leaking space':

> the interval between our perimeter and my threshold is no longer resolute but capricious, determined by shadow and light, formed by a fluidity of both space and time.
>
> (MILLAR 2011: 11)

Where lace and its holes make such leakage visibly apparent, Millar's approach offers a way for thinking back into woven cloth. In setting cloth in terms of holes and threads, the notion of cloth as a shimmering surface can be approached from within its surface. Guiliana Bruno does just this as she considers cloth's surface tension. As a surface for light and as a screen for project, Bruno presents cloth as migratory, provisional and yet manifestly material (2014: 3). With her focus on Robert Irmin's installation *Excursus: Homage to the Square* (1998), Bruno thinks through the passage of light and form across the different screens within the work: canvas, wall, scrim.[1] In this she highlights ways in which images become formed through the surfaces on which they appear to the viewer, modifying and mediating those images in parallel with Millar's lace structures.

Bruno positions the screen as a multilayered surface, with its transformative agency held within the thickness formed by those layers (2014: 75). As light and images permeate and play across the layers, Bruno excavates the shimmering layers. The screen is simultaneously envelope, curtain and screen, flickering between modes, constantly restless.

The idea of cloth as shimmering surface to be excavated layer by layer in the manner of the archaeologist is an approach adopted by Diana Wood Conroy in 'Archives of Cloth: shadows of the past in re-visioning textiles' (in Jefferies, Wood Conroy and Clark 2016: 137–48). Here Wood Conroy emphasizes the 'shadowy flickering nature of the evidence for ancient textiles' (137). Through the use of evocative terminology: 'pseudomorphs' (shapes that form an imprint or cast) and 'skiamorphs' (shapes that shadow other materials) – this text brings together language and materiality at the surface of the 'lost' textile. Through an extended notion of the archive, Wood Conroy reveals ways in which textile and the shadows it casts can offer new readings of cultural pasts. Quoting curator Victoria Lynn, Wood Conroy notes that 'paradoxically the idea of absence is signalled through the material presence of a trace – in the form of text, gesture, blood . . . and a feverish obsession to find fragments of that loss' (Lynn in Jefferies,

Wood Conroy and Clark 2016: 145). Here then Wood Conroy sets textile as a shimmering surface; presence and absence oscillate, restlessly veiling each other, making sense of one another in manner that echoes and extends Millar's capricious lace boundaries.

Veils: A space of scintillation

Let's never forget in the amplifying cave or in the resonating cavity that engenders this radiance, there'll already have been need of two reflecting surfaces, two mirrors parallel to each other and perpendicular to the rays. Two mirrors echo each other in parallel, an echo of light in parallel: *one next to the other.*

(CIXOUS AND DERRIDA 2001: 49)

This text is taken from *Veils* (2001), a dialogue of two texts and accompanying images, through which philosophers Hélène Cixous and Jacques Derrida explore myopia and Cixous' recovery from it. *Veils* is a text that is about the shimmering light of myopia and the veil: between blurred and clear vision and between two writers. In the darkness of myopia Cixous navigated her way, operating within a murky twilight and drawing on the veiled (female) face as a metaphor for her story. Following surgery Cixous sees clearly and so her old self becomes a foreigner and the foreign becomes her new self. Derrida's text echoes, mirrors and weaves around Cixous' veil taking the Jewish talith shawl as its point of reference. In *Veils* Derrida and Cixous establish textile as a metaphor and a language for the shimmering surface of vision:

> You're dreaming of taking on a braid or a weave, a warp or a woof, but without being sure of the textile to come, if there is one, if any remains and without knowing if what remains to come will still deserve the name of text, especially of the text in the figure of a textile.
>
> (CIXOUS AND DERRIDA 2001: 24)

As gendered language hovers within the Cixous–Derrida textual folds, playfully held between the feminine *la voile* (sail) and the masculine *le voile* (veil), so they create a space of scintillation. Cixous' text dances between poetry, fiction and memoir and, in reflecting upon her 'recovery', celebrates its retreat at the same time as mourning its loss. In her previous, myopic, life 'She and Doubt were always inseparable' (6), but now in her 'no-longer-not-seeing' world (9) 'she was discovering the bizarre benefits her internal foreigner' brought 'that she had never been able to enjoy with joy' (12).[2]

As Cixous oscillates and vacillates between the veiled, blurry myopic world and the clear-sighted, corrected-eye world, she is able to 'see both shores' (16) at once and is able to appreciate the benefits and pleasures of each simultaneously. For Derrida's part his meditations upon Cixous' text open up other veilings and unveilings through notions of hidden and revealed truths. As he weaves his narrative, he, too, oscillates between veiling and unveiling, here and there, clear sight and myopia, between life and death, sleep and wakefulness.

Both writers write textile, the veil, but refer to different veils. Together, this is a shimmering cloth that is neither masculine nor feminine, neither purely textile nor text, but oscillates between: shimmering.

The texts begin and end with the silkworm, that secreter of thread, but also, in a mirroring of Cixous' 'veil', the silkworm becomes a moth only through the death of itself. What emerges from these texts is that 'truth' is neither found in the darkness nor in the light, but in the shimmering and oscillating half-light of between: at and on the iridescent surface.

Faintly gleaming

When semi-transparent fabric is layered, very often the passage of light through the woven surface is disrupted and thus a moiré effect is produced. This effect is defined mathematically as an interference pattern created by the overlapping, but slightly misaligned grids. In photography moiré is a form of aliasing which produces false patterning brought about by the spatial arrangements of colour tones being sampled at low resolution. According to E. Ullrich (1929–30), the moiré effect comes about as a result of space between the layers of fabric which 'takes on the characteristics of a "glimmer" or faint "shimmer" similar to the sun reflecting from a rippled water surface' (1930: 1205). Like the play of light on water, the moiré effect that emanates from between the layers of cloth in this way shimmers and moves. With cloth, the movement of both cloth and viewer cause this effect to shift and change and with successive misalignments of the warp–weft grid, the play of light continues to produce a sense of further indefinite movement. Thus, moiré effects are based upon light reflection and the play of light on the threads between the two woven cloths; it is especially visible from a distance, although observable in close proximity in some cases.

Where Ullrich's moiré focuses upon the play of light on the threads within the cloth, Barthes' shimmer is predicated upon the angle of the subject's gaze. Here the shimmer presents a play *between* light and dark, which is not bland nor static, but full of lustre and continuous movement to and fro. Within the moiré effect, the spatial alignment of warps and wefts together with the roundedness of those threads means that the light never settles, producing its ever-shifting patterns.

To locate textile as shimmering surface in relation to both Ullrich's moiré and Barthes' Neutral, it is necessary to first consider how Barthes constructs the

Neutral as an active, affective agent rather than as a muffling or dampening of oscillations. For Barthes,

> the Neutral [is] that which outplays [*déjoue*] the paradigm, or rather I call Neutral everything that baffles the paradigm.
> (BARTHES 1978: 50)

Where, for Barthes, the paradigm is an oppositional structure of exemplar, the Neutral is an active, affecting agent (7). In a similar vein, Julia Kristeva develops the role of poetic language as a meaning-making process, suggesting in her paper 'Word, Dialogue and Novel' (1980)[3] that such language is relational and cannot be reduced to its logical and concrete operations if meaning is to be made. In this relational form, there exists a double aspect within language, which Kristeva asserts has the potential to enable writing to be simultaneously the creation of subjectivity and communication (68). Like Barthes' Neutral, poetic language, in its doubling or shimmering of meaning, defies the oppositional.

Such language reverberates and expands within the doubling. It is a carnivalesque form of language according to Kristeva (72). Such a form privileges relational interplay over fixed structures. Carnivalesque structuring is essentially a dialogical form, within which actor and spectator oscillate between roles, and from within the dialogue language evades linearity in active and creative tension (79).

Where Barthes' Neutral produces a vibrating relationship, Kristeva's carnivalesque language is built upon the suspension of the everyday to enable actor and spectator to occupy one another's perspective and take on their actions. In this space of collapsed hierarchies and binaries, the relational is paramount in its confusion and visceral bodiliness. This aligns with Giorgio Agamben's critique of Barthes' model of the paradigm, which he suggests is 'depolar and not dichtomic', a tensional field which 'thus produces a new ontological context' (Agamben 2002: 4). What Agamben focuses upon is the 'para' or 'shown beside' of paradigm, which emphasizes a provisional and temporal context. Like Kristeva, the collapsed moment exposes a part of the interplay between elements, creating new interactions. This is the moment in which readability parts company with both determined meaning and knowledge in the temporary ontological context. Thus the paradigm, for Agamben, is a singularity known from being shown as one of a field of possibilities.

The paradigm thought of in this way means that Barthes' Neutral is already accommodated within the paradigm, but I would suggest that through Kristeva and Agamben, Barthes' Neutral is extended to include the tensional field of possibilities, the tremulous or flickering that crosses the temporal field to form a 'spatial–temporal constellation' (Agamben 2002: 8). In this sense, then, for the Neutral to outplay the paradigm is to refer to a condition of activity and movement within the tensional field established. The Neutral offers more than a choice between terms, but 'a discourse of the other of choice' (1978: 8). In terms of the textile as shimmering surface, then, the Neutral relocates the relationship between warp, weft, light and space, enabling the interplay between them to become a space of scintillation that shimmers.

Illicit encounters

In order to think further about textile as shimmering surface, in this section I propose to bring together the Neutral as the shimmer with Briony Fer's discussion of Eva Hesse's work, to open out a reading that emphasizes the Neutral as functional, and affecting, rather than conceptual.

I first encountered the work of Eva Hesse in the early 1990s. This was a space of exuberance and power of the materiality. I was immediately drawn to Hesse's shapes and lines that spring from fundamental forms: circles, spheres, loops and rings. Sometimes there was symmetry, sometimes not; they felt bodily, but references were often fleeting. All these were alongside her bold, expressive drawings. As Lucy Lippard wrote of in her monograph on Hesse, 'she seemed to be forming a vocabulary of shapes that longed to be independent of the page' (Lippard 1976: 15).

Elissa Auther points to this forming of vocabulary in terms of Hesse's inventiveness, her ability to extend and extract from her materials (2009: 89). Further, it is Hesse's responsiveness to her materials that gives her work its visceral magnetism. Auther sums this up:

> It was sensual not intellectual, organic not abstract, tactile not verbal, and as Hesse puts it, 'non ... nothing'.
>
> (2010: 91)

Vanessa Corby likewise explores such a material-led approach in Hesse's oeuvre, focusing upon two drawings, and noting her differentiation between the 'sketches', the drawing practice and the sculptural constructions: 'tacit knowledge leads her making' (2010: 16). In this sense, Hesse can be seen to think through her materials, be it charcoal, ink, latex, rubber, cloth, fibre and paint and her production of what she calls 'absurdity' or 'non ... nothing' is, as Corby suggests, 'to register the relationship between materials and bodily movement' (21). Here, drawing on Merleau-Ponty, she positions this relationship as 'an intertwining of vision and movement' (1964b: 127)

In this intertwining of vision and movement, there is an echoing of the way in which textile has the capacity to occupy space, sometimes in terms of mass, but also through implication, allusion and even illusion. This occupation of space extends textile's inherent possibilities: the lines of fibre, but it also offers a way for thinking about textile through its behaviour in such occupation. Hemmings notes that 'textiles, one of the most portable material disciplines, move with such relative ease around our world' (2015: 15) in reference to their ability to offer ways by which to engage in postcolonial thinking. However, to think of this mobility at an intimate level destabilizes the solidity of textile, causing it to oscillate within the tensional field of vision and movement, to shimmer in the light.

The work of Eva Hesse provides a rich field of art practice through which to draw out the notion of the Neutral as shimmer partly as a result of its ability to 'foil one-note readings' (Meyer in Sussman 2006: 62) but also within her work opposites are found working simultaneously. In this sense her work acts out the Neutral through expressive interaction with her materials[5] and thus displaces binaristic approaches in favour of what could be considered to be a form of nomadic or transitional practice. In Hesse 'material presence, that palpable sense of what [her] work was made of, combines so disconcertingly with the sense of a void' (Fer in Gill 2000: 73). Here matter and non-matter, material and space establish a tensional field that together forms a space from which to explore collisions and elisions that occur in the gaps between painting, sculpture and drawing. It is her occupation of this space that makes Hesse such an inspiration within the field of textiles in that she sought to subvert the boundaries between these modes. Hesse did not position herself in relation to textile practice, but her use of materials and her challenge of the borderlines between disciplines make her an important figure to textile practitioners. To read Hesse's work through textile highlights its ability to operate across such boundaries. It must also be noted that there were a number of fibre artists seeking to subvert practices in adjacent ways, such as Lenore Tawney, Magdalena Abakanowicz, Rosemary Mayer, Judith Shea and Ritzi Jacoby.[4] What is important here is the way in which Hesse directly articulates her practice in terms of its logic and possibility and the ways in which it becomes a useful way for thinking about textile as a shimmering surface.

To begin to think about Hesse's work in terms of a shimmering textile practice, I want to start with *Hang Up* (1966): a simple wooden frame bandaged with strips of cloth painted in subtly graduated shades of grey revealing an empty space or void within. Disrupting the structure, a coil of similarly wrapped wire emerges from the frame, trespassing or even capturing the viewer's space in front of the work. Hesse's bandaging fills the void and voids the space, presenting what Pamela Lee calls an 'illicit encounter between pictorial and sculptural space' (Lee 2002). Annette Tietenberg draws attention to the tensional field Hesse interrupts with this work, alluding to Barthes' Neutral:

> Exactly at the moment when painting abandons the field that is traditionally accorded it, it acquires increased room for manoeuvre. It becomes excessive, object like, present, palpable.
> (TIETENBERG QUOTED IN GAßNER, Kölle and Roettig 2013: 191)

In this Hesse playfully challenges the genres as polarized positions, proposing an active, shimmering space between.

While the work has often been compared to, and clearly resonates with, Dan Flavin's open, luminous corner frames and Jasper Johns' empty stretcher *Canvas* (1956) or his wire structures which emanate from the wall such as *No* (1961) or *In Memory of My Feelings* (1961), Hesse's void expresses itself through the way in which the emerging coil interrupts the rectilinear rigidity of Johns' and Flavin's frames, suggesting a bodily swelling that expands the skin from inside, and thus emphasizes the contrapuntal logic between matter and void while also referencing the feminine space of maternity. The swaddled and painted frame articulates the interior space, and yet the interior void, both within the frame and that created by the protruding wire itself, articulates absent planes and surfaces, lending the space a palpability and tensional field of its own.

In terms of textile practices, reading Hesse's work offers a space for thinking about the role of materiality. Looking at her sketchbooks and notebooks it appears that Hesse moved smoothly and to some extent intuitively to and fro between sketching, painting and sculpting, constantly adjusting and experimenting to achieve the forms seen in her 'finished' works. Briony Fer's curation of *Studiowork* (2009) was the result of extensive research into Hesse's studio practices and 'test-pieces', which were staged without protective cases or barriers. The exhibition included small, experimental works or test pieces, which were produced alongside or in advance of her larger-scale sculptural pieces,[5] and together with the broader project demonstrates this oscillation between testing and finishing in that many of the items on display can be seen as elements or part-objects within completed works, sometimes in several so that it is difficult to decipher between the two modes. *Studiowork* (2009) provides invaluable insight into Hesse's working practices in temporarily returning the artist to the work, bringing to life LeWitt's comment on artists' scribbles that 'those that show the thought processes of the artist are sometimes more interesting than the final product' (LeWitt 1969).

Fer notes that categorizing Hesse's work has always been difficult (Fer 2009: 16) and uses the term 'studioworks' because, like the work itself, it is expedient, inclusive but, importantly, elastic. The studioworks are difficult to talk about, and Fer takes great trouble to set out a means for doing so that is not about reducing them to their constituent parts or their resemblances within larger, more complete works, but establishes their wider roles and dialogue within her practice. Fer's text sees her searching for the best methodology for understanding the pieces, a process which evokes Barthes' Neutral in its baffling of the paradigm. Fer is returned time and again to the hands forming the elements, to the thoughts and ideas running through Hesse and yet all the time resisting nomenclature, typologies, linear narratives and even the notion of incomplete/completed works.

These items are provisional, improvised and in process. Fer notes that 'The powerful, if not lethal, mix of matter and sex makes it a volatile thing' (Fer 2009: 21), a description or expression of affect that recalls Kristeva's carnivalesque poetic language, where meaning is made outside of conventions, when hierarchies and boundaries collapse into visceral bodily interplay. Meaning from these studioworks (and indeed many of Hesse's works) emerges or leaks out, and Fer points to the role of the haptic senses involved in understanding them and their strangely intimate language.

Within these 'works' there is the constant reminder of her hand, metaphorically and physically, in the creation of what is seen, but what Hesse achieves is a bringing together of fixed and free-flowing forms that confound both Barthes and LeWitt in this sense and produce work that oscillates between the spaces set out by them. Through what Fer refers to as sub-objects, studioworks that sit on a knife-edge between detritus and art object, between prototype and archetype, but a 'sort of first encounter' (Fer 2009: 188), she denies the viewer singular readings or positionings. It is also clear from Hesse's notebooks and other writings that the almost unfinished quality within her work was part of her intention:

> It is my main concern to go beyond what I know and what I can know. The formal principles are understandable and understood. It is the unknown quantity from which and where I want to go. As a thing, an object, it accedes to its non-logical self. It is something, it is nothing.
> (ARTIST STATEMENT, June 1968, quoted in Lippard 1976: 131)

and again, 'A thing/the thing is made' (quoted in Fer 2009: 188), and in the play between 'a' and 'the', Hesses secretes the process of the studioworks in her practice. Such play between definite and indefinite found in these studioworks is also borne out in other of Hesse's works, creating a space of shimmering surfaces and substance, matter and non-matter, threads and light.

Absurdity

The term 'absurdity' is a repeated theme emerging from Hesse's own writing and thus a term used of her by others, such as Lucy Lippard (1992), Elizabeth Sussman (2006), Elissa Auther (2010), Alison Corby (2010) and Brigitte Kölle (2013). While Lippard suggests that this absurdity is Hesse's wit whose 'jokes have no punch line' (Lippard 1992: 185), I want to suggest here a link between 'absurdity' in Hesse's work and the concept of the shimmer through a focus upon *Metronomic Irregularity II*. This will be further developed to consider textile's ambiguity as a form of absurdity through its shimmering surface.

The work consists of three square panels, each perforated with a grid of holes into which hand-covered wires were seated and linking the three grids together in rhythmic, yet irregular waves. Title and work offer contradiction(s): regularity of grid against and alongside irregularity of wire, regularity of the metronome against and alongside irregularity of form. In many ways the wires, while beginning and ending within the grid, also articulate a space in front of the grid, thus like *Hang Up* they establish an interplay between the dimensional space of painting and of sculpture. Fer suggests that Hesse's work in general 'dramatizes some tendency within minimalism itself, in the realm of the "symbolic" and the formal resistance to "symbols" as such . . . based on an economy of loss' (Fer in Nixon 2002: 58). This economy of loss is to be found in Hesse's own sense of 'nothing' or absurdity. Fer refers to this as 'a kind of blankness' (Fer in Nixon 2002: 58) and James Meyer calls them 'unlikely entities' (Meyer in Sussman 2002: 78). Mel Bochner noted that *Metronomic Irregularity II* 'is not chaos, but a structure ordered in itself yet unavailable to comprehension' (Bochner 1967). In both *Hang Up* and *Metronomic Irregularity II* horizontal, vertical and dimensional space is displaced in favour of the support, a logic taken up by other minimalists. However, Hesse's search for absurdity would also appear to be a drive to create works that consider what she called the object's 'non-logical self'.

The notion of an 'economy of loss' is interesting here as it diverts attention away from content, structure and meaning in the conventional sense, pointing attention as much to what is not physically or immediately present in the work as to what has been retained or included. In terms of thinking about textile as a shimmering surface, this establishes a space for textile's ambiguity. Made up from the arrangement of threads/fibres and spaces, textile hovers or shimmers between threshold and covering, and it is as a result of this shimmering that its crossing is not always known. As light plays across the surface of the cloth and its movement casts the threads in altered perspective, so the loss of substance becomes a potent space for meaning-making.

Elissa Auther considers Hesse's particular use of fibre in her work, noting that while Hesse herself described it in terms of translating the drawn line into real space, fibre enables 'numerous powerful oppositions, such as those between hard and soft, order and chaos, regularity and randomness, vertical and horizontal, solidity and formlessness' (201: 73), producing qualities that lead to the absurd without defining and thus delimiting it as a medium or mode of making.

In this sense Hesse's search for the work's absurdity or non-logical self results in a syntax of materiality that hovers in a sort of limbo: it shimmers between logic and non-logic. One work that highlights this is *Right After* (Plates 5 and 6), which initially resembles a canopy or tent-like space. The work consists of 100- to 200-foot lengths of fibreglass cord that have been dipped into resin and then hung from the ceiling. It is interesting to note here that there exists a drawing from 1969 also entitled *Right After* (Plate 4) that resembles a woven cloth with fringed edging or perhaps a cloth still attached to the loom or frame. In his analysis of the installation, Mark Godfrey compares the way Hesse had it hanging in her studio with only natural side lighting to its staging at the Jewish Museum in 1969 (Plate 6). In the latter venue and more recently at Yale University Art Gallery (1992), harsh overhead lighting rendered greater contrasts of light and shade than the muter and softer lighting of her studio (Plate 5), where 'it could sometimes disappear and become a "really big nothing"' (Godfrey in Sussman 2002: 32).

It is this ability for several hundred feet of resin-soaked cord to disappear and reappear, to shimmer, which is of interest here. The matrixial form hangs like a piece of fabric caught in mid-flight as it falls from ceiling to floor. Like Millar's lace, the spaces or holes of *Right After* offer the contours of its 'whole' as a threshold or ambiguous borderline. *Right After* seems to hover, and Robert Clark writes: 'The mutability of these hanging pieces serves as a metaphor for that which can't be fixed or known, while their physical suspension evokes a kind of psychological suspense' (Clark in Sussman 2002: 274) or suspended animation.

Hesse, commenting on the piece, suggested such provisionality:

> This piece is very ordered. Maybe I'll make it more structured, maybe I'll leave it changeable. When it is completed its order could be chaos. Chaos can be structured as non-chaos.
>
> (QUOTED IN LIPPARD: 172)

To read the work in terms of order, it becomes a woven cloth and places the focus upon the points of connection with the ceiling and its warp–weft structure. In Hesse's work, notions of absurdity, non-logic and provisionality operate in tandem with challenges to materiality of art practice and disciplinary boundaries. These are the paradigms that Hesse's work outplays or baffles. As order, chaos and non-chaos hover between, they produce a tensional field which resists singular reading. Hesse's practice is logic and non-logic, absurd and rational, sculpture, painting and drawing. In its ambiguity, *Right After* animates the rhythms of cloth without becoming such a fixed canopy, veil or covering. The work takes on the play of light across its threads, and light and shade pass through its holes as it shimmers in space.

Through the looking glass

If the shimmer can be thought of in terms of the 'not yet' or even the 'not ever', then it could also be thought of as a means by which the spaces and gaps between and within the textile's holes and threads can secrete and accrete meaning and understanding. An artist whose work expresses these issues is the Canadian Tricia Middleton. Her installations enchant and disgust as they take their forms from found objects, detritus, sometimes recognizable but often not. All the while they mesmerize and enchant the viewer.

Described as 'some strange phantasmagorical stage set' (Marchand 2009: 25), Middleton's works entice and involve the body through a process that collapses spatial landmarks. This work extends, deepens and opens out spatial limitations, while simultaneously drawing them deep within the baroque materiality.

Referencing domestic spaces, household detritus and overconsumption, it is easy on first encountering these works to get caught up in trying to identify the part-objects, to create individual narratives for the elements incorporated, to feel hampered by the swathed fabric, wax, the dust and the decay that threatens to overwhelm. However, it is through being shown beside their reference points that this work strategically addresses scopic dominance in viewing through the very intimacy of the installations in which the bodily, skinly viewer is implicated, even submerged, by the work.

In *Troubles with Boundaries* (2017) (Plates 7 and 8), the loose scattering of draped fabric, wax-covered objects and other matter in these assemblages emphasizes the contingency and particularity of each of the elements together with its reference to ways in which capitalism even finds ways to marketize its own waste. The installation tempers destruction and decay with a sense of exuberance and vitality. Domestic connotations give way to excess, transgression and absurdity. In an echo of Hesse's *Right After* Middleton's *Troubles with Boundaries* not only absorbs the gallery space into its entropic logic but the work becomes dependent upon the exterior spaces. Each piece is in dialogue with the other, rendering the work's surfaces and whole as porous. This is a practice of excess: a sedimented space that overflows in its ambiguity. Textile held in this context comes into this entropic logic, shifting and changing through dialogue.

Beyond this *Troubles with Boundaries* has a through-the-looking-glass quality. Its wax-covered objects, painted and torn fabrics, its threads looping between elements, the veiling and curtaining draw the viewer into its surfaces with the almost recognizable. It then mocks them with their obvious contrivances that set the handmade alongside the mass-produced. Middleton establishes an idiosyncratic intervention that critiques classic representations and collections as objects of visual pleasure.

The draped, painted and torn fabrics operate as a pivot point or threshold between materiality and representation. In locating these within the phantasmagorical, Middleton draws out of them the sense of menace and threat of the 'wild'. As Marchand writes: 'The fathomless regions of the unconscious now come to the surface, through the artist's examination of that which eludes the power of the will: the passage of time, the ephemeral, the transient' (2009: 31).

Middleton's work rejects passivity in vision, bringing materiality to the body, establishing both as sites for shimmering thinking and libidinal investment. This work, like Hesse's, defies and challenges easy apprehension and categorization: in its accumulations it is autobiographical yet universal, sensational yet specular, domestic yet global, playful yet rebellious. This is not to set these up here in Middleton's work as oppositional pairings, rather as nodes on the scintillating matrix of her practice. In this work, the individual parts appear to be trying to hold onto their individual identities. In their amassing they become held within this tensional field. Jake Moore writes:

> Disturbed by the idea of the reduction of art objects into the corpses of capitalism, she [Middleton] suggests that they are more likely the 'undead', rotting and limp, unstable on this plane yet unable to cross over into a place for forgetting.
>
> (MOORE 2005)

Middleton's gathering, assembling, re-pairing, assembling and collaging operates beyond oppositional structures to create work that encourages slippage between elements, oscillation between materiality and fantasy, between desire and disgust, consuming and detritus.

In these works, then, Middleton offers doubling up, over and through the installations: the viewer is brought so close it becomes distorted and then draws back at the point of cognition such that the symbolic order is disrupted and distorted, breaking down subject–object, self–other dualisms. Elements layer over each other, underscoring the doubling beside each other. Images, sounds and textures waiver irresolutely and restlessly, oscillating and shimmering, reflecting one another.

According to Rodolph Gasché, reflection can be considered as 'the process and structure of the mirroring of an object by a polished surface *and*, at the same time, a mirroring of the mirror as well' (Gasché 1986: 20). In this he suggests a doubling movement that occurs within reflection, that establishes a non-polarizing and yet potentially infinite relationship between subject, object and mirroring surface, which here can be thought of in terms of a shimmering surface.

In Middleton's work this doubling creates an excess: it shimmers and oscillates. Like the veil of Hélène Cixous' myopic former life, doubt and uncertainty secrete meaning within these shimmering textile surfaces. 'Myopia shook up everything including the proper peace that blindness establishes. . . . Myopia was her truth' (Cixous and Derrida 2001: 7 and 10). The myopic exists within a liminal world which, while indistinct and murky, is also a realm of dynamic potential – it is a world or realm of infinite possibilities and potentialities within that indistinctness. It is also one in which vision and visioning cannot be the dominating mode of perceiving, veiled as it is.

As a way for thinking about textile practice, the shimmer brings together the dazzling with the murky in terms of visioning and matterliness with secretions of meaning. This is an (inter)relationship which depends upon both clear-sightedness and myopia, textile and production, in their fullness, held together in dynamic tension.

Here, textile as a shimmering surface of tensional fields offers the notion of reflection as an expansion of the space between subject and object, but without separation. In so doing this creates a space of emergence in which the associated notions of reflection and reflexivity become key points of interest.

To think through and beyond the paradigm opens up an indistinct and murky mode for thinking through textile and cloth. In this mode the traditional dominance of the product over process becomes challenged and, through the myopia of the shimmer, both are brought together in a way that does not privilege either, and it does not aim to arrive at a static place in-between. Rather the shimmer as a model for thinking about this interplay within textile practice offers thinking that is initiated within the dynamic of the cloth as both surface and screen, both reflection and object, baffling the paradigm.

3
SEAMING

Repetition, duplication, and alternation are important parameters . . . threads have the ability to create volumes from very little, from almost nothing, from a line.

(RIKE FRANK IN FRANK AND WATSON 2015: 28–9)

Rike Frank, writing in *Textiles: Open Letter* (2015), a project that takes as its focus textile's materiality and, most particularly, the idea that 'the material is always also a medium and thus part of the message' (2015: 7), is concerned with the changing status of textile as a means of analysis within a networked world. Such an approach to analysis, Frank suggests, opens up a space for a contemporary artistic textile practice that departs from multiple sites and with an altered and alterable notion of media (22–59). In this, then, it allows space and breath for the richness and potency of textile to highlight and champion the network as journey: traversing history, society and media. The resultant journey-lines, or threads, move to and fro between elements, concepts and narratives, seaming and joining as they pass.

The idea of making a seam or joining fragments will be considered here primarily as a concept by which to trace a pathway between making and writing (textile and text) and think through them together in the processes of production. This chapter will explore techniques and processes for making seams to create this pathway both metaphorically and literally. In this, seaming will be taken in terms of its capacity to extend the cloth, but will also address aggressive and disruptive aspects of needle and thread passing through the textile.

The status of conjunctions, crossings, edges, boundaries and exchanges will be taken as focal points, thus drawing on precedents such as Janis Jefferies (in Mitchell 2000), Elaine Showalter (1988), Victoria Mitchell (2013), Pajaczkowska (2007), T'ai Smith (2015) and Paula Owen (in Buszek 2011). These ideas will be extended by tracking a route from the technicalities of the processes involved in making seams through to think through a methodological model for writing and thinking *about* textile practice within an expanded field of visual culture. Artworks by Ann Hamilton and Kirstie Macleod will be focused upon within this discussion and ways in which their practices evoke and invoke seaming, both metaphorically and through material means.

The American literary critic Elaine Showalter in her paper 'Piecing and Writing' looked to the practice of quilting, particularly patching and piecing techniques, as a way to understand American women's writing. In this essay, which has recently been republished in both *The Textile Reader* (Hemmings 2012a: 157–70) and *Textile: Critical and Primary Sources* (Harper 2012: 203–20), Showalter identifies three phases of work: piecing or sewing together fragments of fabric, patching or joining units together, and quilting or attaching the patchwork to its backing. She establishes parallels between these and written language, namely the sentence, the structure of the story or novel, and the imagery or symbolism used. Quoting art critic Lucy Lippard, Showalter asserts that 'the quilt has become the prime visual metaphor for women's lives, for women's culture', suggesting quilting as an expression of 'the pre-verbal semiotic phase of mother–child bonding' (1988: 227). Taking an approach that mirrors patching and piecing with the narrative traditions of American women's writings, Showalter highlights ways in which fragmented time, repetition and the building together of the whole operate within these frameworks. She builds a compelling scaffold for women's writing in which blocks of memory, flashbacks, repetition, melancholy, joy, irregularity and recycling become strategies for an open-ended and potentially unfinished model for writing, a model which allows for and celebrates the potential for ongoing patching, piecing and recycling.

Janis Jefferies, textile writer, curator and artist, suggests that such thinking in terms of piecing and joining has the potential to operate as a form of subjective self-positioning for women, a mode by which contemporary textile practice can be considered in terms of a system of mobile entities seeking to transgress borders and boundaries. Such boundaries, constructed upon certitude and knowledge, can be challenged, suggests Jefferies, through the performance of a double paradox of dislocation and fixity found in the coalescence between woman and textiles. She argues that such transgression can be achieved through a strategic 'autographics' of hybridity: a form of thinking and writing that takes the form of tactical, and sometimes playful, self-invention.

Jefferies draws on Jeanne Perreault's notion of autographics as a mode for writing the self that is based upon flexibility and transformation, that is, the flexible self is transformed in writing as the self it changes (Perreault 1995). In this there are parallels with Luce Irigaray's 'productive mimesis', a mode of self-performing that enables woman 'to try to recover the place of her exploitation . . . by an effect of playful repetition' (Irigaray 1977: 73–4).

Such an approach plants an important marker here in that it opens out a space for transience, transgression and a challenging of patriarchal models of selfhood. Through this Jefferies suggests that the conjoint roles of autography and textile have the potential to operate as a means by which to construct identity beyond notions of assimilation and fixity of meaning (Jefferies in Bachmann 1998: 14–21).

To write autographically, according to Jefferies, is to identify with a female imaginary: a space of productive incoherence which resists 'final, conceptual or material closure' (in Jefferies, Conroy Wood and Clarke 2016: 44). In this sense boundaries and edges become a site for seaming and joining the fragments, forming an ever-changing, provisional subjectivity

Taking a slightly different tack, Claire Pajaczkowska considers, in 'Thread of Attachment' (2007: 140–53), the role of string and thread not only for doing things, functional operations, but also for being: as being related. In this she focuses upon the transitions made between being, feeling, seeing, knowing and thinking and the ways in which writing can trace that system of transfer, or transition, from body to thought. By placing the process of making with string at the forefront of her thinking, Pajaczkowska frames ways by which making becomes a strategic mode for traversing the notion of linear narrative in favour of a multidirectional pathway, one with breakages and interruptions that become integral and vital to the journeying. Likewise, her text takes such a journey from knitting through to shoelaces and cats' cradle games, to twisting and plying, ribbons, ligatures and knots. In this she draws together strands of meaning, concluding with the denouement: that point at which

> the narrative threads are drawn together and at which the unresolved tension of not knowing' becomes a point of eruption of knowledge. This is not a knowing based upon hierarchical, linear systems of logic, but rather a knowing that emerges from the seaming together of multiple fragments, different pathways brought together by the string/thread into a new, enlarged fragment: a form of story-cloth. (Pajaczkowska 2007: 141–52)

Victoria Mitchell similarly evokes such thinking, both in her republished essay 'Textiles, Text & Techne', which opens *The Textile Reader* (Hemmings 2012a: 5–13) and which features in Harper's *Textiles: Critical and Primary Sources* (2012), but also in a another essay 'Stitching With Metonymy' (Mitchell 2013: 315–19). In these texts Mitchell brings to the fore the interplay between writing about textile and making with textile, drawing on linguistic tactics to explore modes of 'speaking through stuff' (2013: 316). Mitchell draws here on Lacan's anchoring point of the free-floating signifier/signified relationship to highlight how the stitch and stitching offer ways not only to understand the workings of metaphor and metonymy but also as 'a metaphorical action, a metaphor of a metaphor' (317). Thus, she establishes the ideas that stitching and seaming can be considered as that which is inserted between saying and meaning, the workings that bring about comprehension. Mitchell frames the activity of stitching as a way of knowing 'that emphasizes textile as an activity of becoming rather than textile as technique or as a realm of objects' (318), something she calls 'to textile'. This activity is thus performative, active and a form of agency that brings about signification not as the shadow or parallel to writing, but as a form of meaning-making-in-process: always provisional, always shifting, a knowing-by-parts.

In order to make this departure, I have structured this chapter around three aspects for thinking about the seam. Seaming as passage: a mode for thinking about seaming as a bodily process, a form of gestation, that draws upon Cixous and the notions of both seaming and writing as performative activities; seaming as suturing: by which to consider ways in which the thickening or overlap between sutured elements secretes meaning within the extended structure; and seaming as trace: in which there is a focus upon agency and its role in bringing-into-being, where the trace of that activity opens up the possibility of different legibilities.

Seaming as Passage

The artist Ann Hamilton writes:

> My first hand is my sewing hand. A line of thread drawn up and down through cloth influences how I think about the confluence and rhythms of space and time.
>
> (ANN HAMILTON)[1]

The simple utilitarian straight stitch can be used to patch, repair, connect and hold fabric pieces together, the needle passing back and forth between them. This term 'back and forth' indicates a mutual exchange brought about by the action of needle and thread, suggesting openness and engagement between pieces. Back and forth implies repetition and rhythm, notions that are most commonly associated with a sense of well-being, perhaps even a meditative state.

What I want to focus upon here is the balance between what stitching does and what stitching can become as a productive or metaphoric element in the joining together of pieces: the passage between. I want to explore ways in which this stitching between, both by hand and machine, joins and connects pieces and fragments together, to create new, expanded pieces. This is not a linear model, but rather a process that champions differences and fragmented paths. To quote material theorist and historian, Peter Stallybrass, the stitch, like other elements within a cloth economy, is 'richly absorbent of symbolic meaning'

(Jones and Stallybrass 2001: 39), a means by which meaning comes into being not as didactic, but rather by parts and inferences.

As a joining mechanism, the stitch could be thought of as operating as a form of translation within a realm of symbolic meaning. This is not translation in terms of swapping or exchanging like for like, but in terms of the drawing together of cultures and cultural understandings. In the same way as the translator cannot simply take a package of words from one language and supplant it, into another without any acknowledgement of cultural contextualization, so the stitcher needs to understand both pieces of fabric, their properties and behaviours, such that the stitching used is figured and fashioned accordingly between them. The stitcher and stitch operate within the double world of the translator, something Sarat Maharaj refers to as a 'perfidious fidelity' (Hall and Maharaj 2001: 31) or untrustworthy faithfulness. As needle and thread pass through the cloth fragments, bringing them together, the fragments remain in relationship but do not *become* each other. They move together, but only while the stitches remain intact. The stitch then becomes a syntactical tool to the translator, fixing meaning within the particular context set, but always with the potential to disband the relationship and become unstitched.

In the creation of the expanded cloth through stitching, there comes together within the passage of the seam both the translatable and the untranslatable, those cultural references that remain within that cultural space. So, where in British English the expression for great hunger is 'I could eat a horse', an expression which references the capacity of that hunger, in French, the closest equivalent is '*j'ai une faim de loup*' (I have the hunger of a wolf), which references the voracity of that hunger. Furthermore, the English expression refers to the British horror of horsemeat as a human foodstuff and the French to the image of a wolf waiting in the woods ready to pounce upon and devour its prey. Thus, the translation is faithful to the localized meaning, but does not carry original cultural contextualization.

As needle and thread make their passage between the two pieces of cloth, that which is directly translatable tracks back and forth between them while the untranslatable elements remain on their 'own' side, but traces of these do pass between, suggesting a sort of veiled supplement to understanding and meaning. I can know what the French equivalent expression is without fully understanding as a French citizen would, the fuller cultural, historical and fabled understanding of the wolf as imagery, grounded as I am within British wolf–horse understandings and imagery. Thus, in French wolf stands as signifier of hunger, whereas in Britain it is the horse: two signifiers, one signified – hunger. Likewise, the French citizen of the British idiom. In this sense then, seaming brings alongside each other two, culturally located, sets of signifier–signified relationships, highlighting differences and similarities between the fabric pieces. To seam a high stretch fabric such as silk jersey to a more rigidly structured kind, such as cotton twill, requires either that the first be carefully positioned such that the stretch is minimized within the seaming and so the twill dictates the space of the seam or that the jersey is allowed to stretch along the length of the twill, which becomes a supporting structure for the flow of the jersey. What is seen here is a materialization of what Derrida refers to as 'a regulated transformation of one language by another, of one text by another' (Derrida 2004: 19), of one cloth by another. This regulated transformation enables, through the passage of the seam, fragments of text, or part-texts, to be held together. The model of the seam, however, ensures that this is not a rigid join, but rather it is flexible and malleable, each piece offering veiled supplements to the other. As the seams used to construct clothing or coverings wrap themselves around the contours of the body or substructure, so too does the seam as regulated transformation wrap itself around the contours of the two, culturally located, sets of language.

In considering this further, it is useful to think about different forms of stitch used for making seams. When hand-stitching the running-stitch becomes readily supplanted by the backstitch, for its added strength and flexibility. The strength of this stitch arises from its construction, which is a circular motion of needle and thread passing forwards and backwards to form a continuous connection on both sides, between the two pieces. In terms of the notion of Maharaj's 'translatable and untranslatable' and Derrida's 'regulated transformation', what the backstitch offers is a model in three dimensions: back and forth between the pieces and to and fro along the line of the stitch, such that revisions, omissions and clarifications are given space. In this the backstitch becomes a model for the exchange of meaning that operates across different levels: direct translation and further cultural contextualization. As the needle and thread make their first passage between the pieces, immediate equivalents are established; with the second passage, the culturally located signifier–signified relationship is further developed such that '*j'ai une faim de loup*' becomes firstly 'I have the hunger of a wolf' and then 'I could eat a horse'. This is materialized in the visible structure of the backstitch: on the one side a seemingly constant row of simple stitches can be seen, while on the other, the pattern of to-ing and fro-ing reveals the repeated passage of signifier–signified relationships between the two.

Within this passage between signifiers and signifieds, names, objects and meanings form a fluid relationship with each other such that, hunger, wolf, horse, capacity and voracity all coexist and co-mingle, albeit momentarily.

This fluidity that precedes the subsequent stabilization of these relationships leaves them forever changed by the process. The stitch, in anchoring the relationship, not only brings the pieces together but in so doing it permanently affects change on each of the pieces involved. Thus, within the space of the stitch, there resides potential for the stitch to become both signifier and signified. In its role as the holding and joining mechanism between pieces, the stitch offers the notion of translating, or stitching, as a field of possibilities. This field is structured around shifting or floating sets of meanings, which when thought of together expand the fabric of language and understanding, rather than foreclosing within a rigid regime in which each language resides in its own separate and separated sphere.

Hand and machine stitching

The fundamental difference between hand stitching and machine stitching is caught up with the action of needle and thread. With hand stitching, the whole needle passes completely through the fabric, is turned and then returns a small distance away, thus forming a single, traceable path between the two pieces. On the other hand, a machine-stitched seam is composed of two threads, one above and one below the pieces to be joined. In this case the needle tip passes through the fabric and is then withdrawn through the same space, catching the lower thread in a loop and creating an intertwining of the two threads. The machine-stitched seam at first appears to be a continuous line of thread, only revealing itself as a series of penetrations and withdrawals on closer inspection. The stitches are seen collectively before being seen individually, thus emphasizing the idea of repetition both as the individual act or action recurred and as the result of these multiple acts brought together to form a collective. In *Difference and Repetition* (1968), Deleuze draws on Nietzsche's concept of the repeated action as 'beginning and beginning again' (136), suggesting a reiteration that allows for renewal. Walter Benjamin, on the other hand in his essay 'The Work of Art in the Age of Mechanical Reproduction' (1936), sees repetition as a form of copying or impoverished replication and as such considers that it negates notions of uniqueness and originality (213). In terms of the line of machine stitches, I want here to consider how the repeated action oscillates in the passage-space between reinvention and sameness. One single machine stitch is ineffectual and useless: it unravels and falls apart whereas with each repeated stitch, the row holds itself together more firmly and the seam or join is achieved.

Thus, this line of momentary penetrations, withdrawals and intertwining of the two threads through the fabric, results in a seaming that, unlike the translation or passing between of the hand-stitched seam, offers a model of bringing together through the process of lamination. In this the two threads effectively trap the fabric pieces together between them to create a layered structure, with the potential for multiple passages or routes between.

The idea of the seam as a lamination can be thought of through the lens of Roland Barthes, who suggests lamination as a system for understanding and building associations, or perhaps patching and piecing. In this Barthes described the photograph as a 'laminated object whose two leaves cannot be separated without destroying them both' (Barthes 1981: 6). Such a system proposes a means for extending pieces through juxtapositions, whereby relationships are built upon proximity and shared space. Within this space all elements (fabrics and threads) collaborate with each other, lending and borrowing and thus mingling their unique properties and behaviours to build an expanded matrix or field of meaning, within and beyond the passage between.

Thinking semiotically lamination unpicks fixed one-to-one signifier–signified relationships, making way for an even more fluid form of meaning-making built upon many-to-one forms: metaphor and metonymy. In the same way as the photograph is simultaneously an image of an object, an object and a narrative, so with metaphoric language layers of potential meaning create a passage or space between signifieds and signifiers, such that they cannot be separated from each other without destroying or irreparably damaging it. The language of the metaphor operates obliquely, such that the expression 'a silken voice' does not mean that the voice in question shares every quality with silk cloth, but rather it is smooth and comforting and with a certain richness associated with the feeling of silk upon the skin. The metaphor allows the fuller qualities of the words both as sounds and as meaning-making units to linger, thus expanding their potential beyond their literal usage and meaning. The passage of meaning, like the stitching threads, holds such multiple meanings together so that understanding becomes both corporeal and cerebral: meaning-making through and in the passage.

The machine-stitched seam, unlike its hand-stitched counterpart, is not so much about binding and drawing through, but about bringing two (or indeed more) pieces together through an intertwining of the sewing threads. This fundamental difference in construction mirrors the difference between the role of the maker's body in the process of stitching. Louise Bourgeois, talking about her stitched works or elements, says of hand stitching:

> The beauty of sewing is precisely in the fact that things can be done and undone without damaging the fabric. . . . [It] has to do with binding and stitching things together. It is a prevention against things being separated. The form and the process must always be connected to the psychological.
> (BOURGEOIS IN SONNENBERG 2006: 36–9)

The hand-stitch then is formed from a single, unbroken thread passed to and fro (and back and forth) between the two pieces by the needle, the whole ensemble held within that intimate bodily space framed by head, lap, torso and arms. In this space, perhaps a maternal space, both nurture and rupture occur and in this sense, it could be said to be the site of the semiotic chora where both complete union with, and reflection of, the mother co-reside in bodily sensations. Julia Kristeva's notion of the semiotic chora suggests a space of mother–infant communication before the symbolic structuring of language, before signifiers become the dominant reference point. Entry into the language-based symbolic order necessitates a splitting, or rupturing, of the mother–infant unity. Binding and stitching by hand could be thought of in terms of invoking the potency of the unified mother–infant realm: in the production of the seam the creative drive and that which is created are brought together and through this recover the semiotic chora.

Thinking in terms of the passage of needle and thread, the space of hand-seaming offers a form of meaning-making that is about access and egress. For Irigaray, this notion of a passage between echoes the process of birthing and giving birth, that inextricable link between mother and child. Existence, then, begins with encounter: two before one. A form of seaming.

For Cixous writing is a bodily process and writing the passage is like giving birth:

> There is a long time and a short time . . . There is gestation and giving birth
> (CIXOUS 1998: 119)

As needle and thread pass to and fro between fabric pieces, turning and tracing the passage between them, so the fragments become extended and the seams shape and form the larger construction through that process.

The machine-stitched seam on the other hand intertwines and laminates beyond bodily confines, joining without retrieving the chora, and thus offers a model that could be considered progressive and generative rather than perhaps the more reparative of hand-stitched seaming.

As the mechanized needle passes up and down through the pieces of cloth, the dog-feed moves the cloth onwards to receive the needle and so the machine-worked seam resists a return to the pre-linguistic. In this sense machine stitching operates within a regime based upon proximity and juxtaposition. This is a regime that foregrounds multiple, diverse and shifting signifier–signified relationships: a passage towards each other. Like Barthes' photograph, the machine-stitched seam is simultaneously a join, the process of joining and an intertwined relationship of proximity.

When considered in terms of a passage between or a passage towards, seaming highlights the productive potential of such a process-space. The passage between could be said to highlight the separateness and difference of the fragments seamed together: in many ways the seam creates or foregrounds an edge.

Showalter's point about patching and piecing as a model for women's writing is precisely that: it is in the passages between fragments, within the seaming space, that meaning and understanding can be generated. Seaming, then, offers a model for thinking-through-making that is not about explaining techniques and processes, but rather about the passages between them. Thus, there is a play between separateness and contiguity within the seam space.

Irigaray suggests that there exists an economy of the passage and an economy of how to pass through it (Irigaray and Gill 1985: 246–7). In this she establishes a space in which two are conjoined while remaining distinct, in touch through proximity and sharing of space along the seam, but not one. The seaming space is foregrounded by these two concepts of proximity and contiguity rather than sameness and in so doing models Irigaray's passage as transformative and generative rather than repetitive and replicating. There is a disorienting doubling and reversing within the passage of the seam space: this crucial space of production between elements commonly resides within the structure, but the effects of its efficiency appear on the visible surface; similarly in producing the seam, the passage of needle and thread to and fro, back and forth bring the passage into physical being.

Thus, process and structure take on a renewed temporal relationship within the seam space and notions of origin and primacy become decentred in favour of contiguity. Here the repeated act of stitching is not established upon the concept of 'original' and 'copy', but rather where all stitches are simultaneously original and copies.

This confusion between the two makes it meaningless to think in terms of an original or first stitch. The one single stitch holds the fragments together at a single point on the surface of each, like Lacan's *point de capiton* (upholstery button) to enable fractional stability, or the temporary sense of meaning (Lacan 1966: 303).

However, a seam makes a join along a line, creating the seaming space or a passage between cloths through the activity of needle and thread passing to and fro, back and forth between them. The seam with its repeated action is concerned with forming and shaping, proximity and contiguity: it expands and extends.

Such an inversion and disruption of the relationship between copy and original that characterizes the topography of the seam offers a way by which to consider seaming as a transgressive act in that it inverts, multiplies and transposes, refusing passivity and surrender to the new surface created. Instead it operates as a form of speculum, generating multiple reflections in multiple directions. Subject and object, copy and original, mirror and image pass to and fro between themselves, confusing and disorienting, creating and reproducing themselves within the passage of the seam.

Seaming as suturing

Words were a silver thread stitching the night.
The first story I said led to the light.

(CAROL ANN DUFFY 2012: 8)

There is something inherently ambiguous about the seam: at the same time as it brings two or more pieces of cloth together, it sets them apart. It functions both as an extending mechanism, while also as a limit. The seam conceals and asserts the raw edge of the fabric, the space between the pieces, a crevice, a suture, a scar.

In this section I want to consider the space of that suture also known as the seam allowance, the extra border of cloth that is built into the planning and structure of the seam. T'ai Smith, in her essay 'Three Figures, Three Patterns, Three Paradigms' (2015), notes that this seam allowance is one of the markings on the paper sewing pattern, offering the seamstress 'a device, a functional tool that helps [her] arrive at a specified form . . . a schematic ground for measuring, cutting and connecting pieces of fabric' (4). Through these markings the abstract, flat fabric becomes transformed to work with the body, taking on a new topological form through the ensuing seaming.

As the seam is formed by stitches made a small distance from the raw edge, so the seam allowance is created which becomes hidden from view, but in fact creates a space of thickening, rendering the surface stronger and possessing a new density. This is a new point of juncture where there was separatedness and lesion. Cixous addresses this in the preface to her text *Stigmata: Escaping Texts* (1998), a set of essays in which she focuses upon the processes, perhaps even the *techne,* of writing and the potential for drawing upon different voices and modes by which to form expression. In this she declares that all of the texts within are the result of an injury:

> The texts collected and stitched together, sewn and resewn in this volume share the trace of a wound. They were caused by a blow, they are the transfiguration of a spilling of blood, be it real or translated.
>
> (CIXOUS 1998: XI)

and again:

> All literature is scarry. It celebrates the wound and repeats the lesion . . . scar adds something: a visible or invisible fibrous tissue that really or allegorically replaces a loss of substance which is therefore not lost but added to.

In order to develop these ideas, it is useful here to think about the seam allowance in terms of Gilles Deleuze's 'montage interstice', which he identifies in terms of the cinematic cut and splice:

> What counts is . . . the *interstice* between images, between two images. . . . It is the method of BETWEEN, 'between two images'. . . . It is the method of AND, 'This and then that', which does away with all the cinema of Being = is.
>
> (DELEUZE 1989: 179–80)

In thinking about the seam allowance in these terms, as the *interstice*, there is the sense that the cloth pieces are simultaneously separated and conjoined, and thus seaming represents a liminal process: a threshold between. In crossing to and fro between the pieces of cloth, needle and then thread appear to alter and suspend time and meaning between them. They are joined and yet there has been no elision nor merging, but rather a bringing into proximity, a thickening that foregrounds Deleuze's notion of 'the method of AND' (1989: 180).

> Can you read it? Do you understand? By squares, by inches, you are drawn in. Your fingers read it like Braille.
> History, their days, the quick deft fingers. Their lives recorded in cloth.
> A universe here, stitched to perfection. You must be the child-witness,
> You are the only survivor.
> (JOYCE CAROL OATES, *Celestial Timepiece: Poems. 1980*)

Rachel Blau duPlessis suggests women's writing as a 'verbal quilt' in which 'the materials [are] organised into many centres' (in Showalter 1988: 278), but in focusing upon seaming as sutured scar, duPlessis' idea of the quilt as a counter-hierarchical structure proposes the role of the seam allowance not simply as a mechanism for joining but as the site for an 'anti-authoritarian ethics' (279). In this duPlessis and Showalter are framing structures based upon time rather than meta-narratives, short sections or even fragments brought together, juxtaposed and with their edges held firmly within the space of the suture and allowed to mingle and co-respond as scar tissue.

In many ways the space of the suture could be thought of in terms of the montage, a technique used in film editing in which short clips or stills are spliced together to produce a compressed sequence of information. As such this becomes a space within the film that is thickened. Soviet filmmaker and theorist Sergei Eisenstein suggests that montage foregrounds the spectator and allows for extension here to duPlessis' reader:

> The strength of montage resides in this, that it includes in the creative process the emotions and mind of the spectator. The spectator is compelled to proceed along that self same creative road that the author travelled in creating the image. The spectator not only sees the represented elements of the finished work, but also experiences the dynamic process of the emergence and assembly of the image just as it was experienced by the author.
> (EISENSTEIN 1947: 35–6)

In this, Eisenstein notes that in the sutured film, the process of montage continues to hold that which is no longer visible between them. That space between, known as the 'gutter', stimulates the viewer's eye, mind and imagination, retaining engagement through absence or invisibility. Thinking of the space of the seam in these terms sets it as the repository of both association and differentiation, returning again to Deleuze's 'AND'.

I do not want to suggest that piecing and montage replace seamless and stable narrative forms with a range of free-floating, unrelated elements, cobbled together. Rather, piecing offers a way to bring different and differing voices together and alongside one another, the seams marking flexible points of juxtaposition and the seam allowances thickened, scarred spaces for mutual exchange, a space within the process of translation in which meaning becomes oblique, multiple and mutable. The sutured scar becomes a new place for departure that links but does not direct – a site for duPlessis' 'anti-authoritarian ethics'.

Guiliana Bruno, in *Surface: Matters of Aesthetics, Materiality and Media* (2014), suggests such suturing can be seen in Bill Morrison's film *Decasia* (2002). Through the stained, decayed and spliced (found) film fragments together with their splutterings, bleeds and blurs, there emerges a sequence where textile process and filmic process coalesce as spinners and weavers are seen working within an artisanal factory. The splices, joins and sutures demonstrate the seam as an actively fashioning join, which Bruno suggests is a form of tailoring. In the sutures of the splice, the materiality *of* the film and *in* the film come together, offering ways of thinking-through-the-surface beyond language.

The Argentinian poet and writer Jorge Luis Borges considered language to be a map searching for its territory (1946). In its efforts to draw boundaries, it always falls short as the words are not the thing, but signifiers for that thing. In other words, language seeks to bridge the gap between *what* we know and *how* we know it, or explicit and tacit knowledge.

The work of the artist Ann Hamilton approaches this gap repeatedly through variable forms of practice. In so doing, she creates a pieced landscape of visuality, sensory awareness and language. Like Borges' short story 'On Exactitude in Science' (1946) and duPlessis' essay, 'For the Etruscans' (in Showalter 1988: 271), and Bruno's meditation upon Morrison's *Decasia* Hamilton's constructed environments and installations consist of elements brought together that reflect both human and natural systems and patterns of growth: they are, using Deleuzean terms, rhizomatic. In this sense, then, Hamilton's work is as much concerned with the processes of its fabrication as it is with the 'completed' installations. Thinking in this way of an extended understanding of fabrication positions the work alongside Eisenstein's framework of 'montage'. Hamilton speaks of her practice:

> Cloth, like human skin, is a membrane that divides an interior from an exterior. It both reveals and conceals. It can surround or divide. In its making, individual threads of warp are crossed successively by individual threads of weft. Thus, cloth is an accumulation of many gestures of crossing which, like my gestures

of accumulation, retain an individual character while accreting to become something else.

(HAMILTON 1999: 16)

This accretion and accumulation, layering and montage, create a space between and within the elements, a form of container where the notions and processes of joining are brought to the fore. Like the sutured lesion, Hamilton's works become sites of polymorphous eroticism, a space for undifferentiated, partial and yet enveloping, experiences of materiality.

In order to think about this further, I want to focus upon Hamilton's *human carriage* (2009), installed in the Rotunda of the Guggenheim Museum as part of the exhibition: 'The Third Mind: American Artists Contemplate Asia, 1860 – 1989' (Munroe and Nakagawa 2009) (Plate 9). The work was described on the gallery label as

> a mechanism that traverses the entire Guggenheim balustrade, taking the form of a white silk 'bell carriage' with Tibetan bells attached inside. As the cage spirals down, along the balustrade, the purifying bells ring, awakening viewers. The mechanism is hoisted back up to a post at the uttermost Rotunda Level 6, where an attendant exchanges weights composed of thousands of cut up books that counter the pulley system that propels the mechanism itself.

Such a description of the work covers all of the essential information, but fails to suggest the beauty, playfulness, imagination and ingenuity of the work. As the bells, in their cloth 'tent', wind their way down the Rotunda, ringing gently as they pass, the piece at once both occupies the entire central space and yet is seemingly intimate. This is a work about reading, transmission and transformation of information and ways in which these processes affect or even infect the reader forever. It speaks of latent content accreted and then secreted within the reader to be refound at some later stage and recombined in new ways. Hamilton reflects upon reading:

> What I love about the experience and process of reading is being immersed; the falling into the fold between two pages, the being in the completely 'somewhere else' that is the book. This ability to simultaneously be both here and far away, to be both inside and outside parallels the condition of being a body; it is no surprise the book is the central artifact of culture.

(LEE 2013)

In *human carriage* the seemingly simple becomes increasingly scarry: the sutured lesions forming thickenings and augmentations. There are the prayer bells sliding their way around and around, down and down, taking in each of the levels of the museum, intermittently calling attention to themselves as they pass over the 'triggers' (Plates 9 & 10). Traditionally such bells mark the beginning and end of meditation, acting as space clearers and helping the mind to become free of negative thoughts. In this installation the bells create a gentle moment of rupture in the viewers' contemplations around the whole gallery space and act as metaphor for the nuggets of information held within the body and mind after reading: not the whole, but partial fragments that can be reconnected. There are slices of books, gathered randomly into bundles which act as counterweights to the bells. These bundles of disconnected pieces of information suggest ways in which reading accumulates within each individual and the build-up of knowledge from different sources becomes the counterweight to the quiet and solitary act of reading. Hamilton suggests it is a 'trade-off between what we know through language and what we know through our tactile, sensory experience' (Ayers 2009). There are the silk flags creating a tent around the bells as they float past the viewers on their descent and then another around the 'landing stage'. The Tibetan tradition of hanging flags is an ancient one and marks the sending out of prayers for peace, compassion and wisdom onto the wind, white representing air as one of the five elements. The delicate habutai silk used here in *human carriage* serves to emphasize the spread of knowledge from secreted reading, but as it flutters according to changes in the atmosphere within the building as well as with its movement downwards, the live nature of each passage is emphasized. Each individual performance of the bells from top to bottom mirrors individual acts of reading. The silk offers the viewer a visual cue to that individuality, marking the passage of time and pace of reading the text, making them materially present, with each of their individuations.

In *human carriage* Hamilton offers a spare and yet pregnant space that enables the viewer to contemplate ideas of reading, language, secretion of knowledge and the passage of meaning between bodies and texts. Hamilton often cites Susan Stewart as an inspiration within her work, and in *On Longing* Stewart writes of reading:

> Although reading may give form to time, it does not count in time; it leaves no trace, its product is invisible. The marks in the margin of the page are the marks of writing, not the marks of reading. Since the moment of Augustine's reading silently to himself, reading has inhabited the scenes of solitude: the attic, the beach, the commuter train, scenes whose profound loneliness arises only because of their proximity to a tumultuous life which remains outside their peripheries.
>
> (STEWART 1993: 14)

Here, then Hamilton materializes the irrevocable distance that Stewart describes, between writer and reader, experience and memory. Through the installation she gives form to the seemingly impossible space between language and the material world, not as a mirroring of either or both, but as part-objects and partial forms. In this she opens up knowing as fragmentary and evasive, greater than language, residing between the fragments and within the seam allowance and suturing together of them both.

The Rotunda space within the Guggenheim Museum carves a path through the gallery, creating fissures and gaps which reveal glimpses across and through. As the viewer approaches each individual work they do so through a process that could be likened to an archaeological investigation, layer by layer revealing new artworks. Simultaneously the balustrade and the walkway of the Rotunda operate as forms of suture or stitching of the gallery, creating a pieced whole. It is within this suture-cum-fissure that *human carriage* offers an impression of suspension and expansion of space and time within this contradiction.

Hamilton reflects upon the activity of reading:

> What happens when you read? So often we read out of context or misread things, and I started wondering how you could trace the influence of a particular line or section of text as it passes through all the other things you're reading and being influenced by. How do you account for an influence that comes through a process that changes you forever but doesn't leave a physical trace?
>
> (HAMILTON IN AYERS 2009)

In this sense Hamilton, through *human carriage*, creates a metaphorics or poetics of reading, which actively marks the slippage that exists between language (signifier) and referent (signified). In so doing, this work establishes the activity of reading as a form of deviation from exactitude, highlighting the abstract nature of language. Reading, thought of in this way, draws attention to the different potentialities of the book: as an object, as a set of surfaces, as an abstraction of thought and as a crucible for new knowledges. Returning to Stewart:

> The metaphors of the book are metaphors of containment, of exteriority and interiority, of surface and depth, of covering and exposure, of taking apart and putting together. To be 'between covers' – the titillation of intellectual or sexual reproduction. To be outside the cover, to be godlike in one's transcendence, a transcendence of beginning collapsed into closure, and, at the same time, to be 'closed out'.
>
> The closure of the book is an illusion largely created by its materiality, its cover. Once the book is considered on the plane of its significance, it threatens infinity.
>
> (STEWART 1993: 37–8)

The post-structuralist project of *écriture féminine* is founded upon the principles of such extra-narrativity, space that could be said to foreground the performative, processual and part-known. In suggesting that all texts are the result of an injury, or scarry, Cixous proposes a mode of and for textual production that can be thought of as 'works of being'. This offers a mode that celebrates the fragmented, incomplete and the matrix of connectivities created between artist, maker, writer and the viewer or reader of such production.

Thinking of such connections and connecting, the sutured seam becomes a model which celebrates the scar or seam allowance as a thickened space where tacit and communicable knowledge and understanding come together: a space that champions and encourages signifier–signified slippage.

Seaming as Trace

> Don't put up my Thread and Needle—
> I'll begin to Sew
>
> . . .
>
> Leave my Needle in the furrow—
> Where I put it down—
>
> (DICKINSON in JOHNSON 1976: 617)

In this poem, Emily Dickinson writes a form of meditation upon the practical and performative act of sewing, offering a focus for considering the relationship between performance and language through the stitching with threads. Thinking in terms of text/textile relationships it is useful here to turn to Julia Kristeva's study of the interplay between language and the body; an interplay that thinks of a textile-body together and in combination with its text:

> The body, moreover, is the place where we 'are' as speaking beings; it is the place of material support of the language of communication.
>
> (KRISTEVA IN LECHTE 1990: 53)

In this sense, then, constructing a text could be thought of in terms of a performance between paper, agency and the human body, the text remaining as the trace of that performance. Luce Irigaray refers to this trace as morphology, the study of the form of words and their parts: which opens up a notion that the meaning of such works and their parts are provisional and specifically located.

Thus Irigaray posits the performance of writing, or bringing into being of the text-as-trace, as a performance that Robinson suggests is 'never complete or completeable' (in Irigaray and Whitford 1991: 97–8). Such a morphology of incompleteness involves what Irigaray calls 'mimesis as production' (1991: 134). This is a mimicry by woman who plays with ideas about herself, through her bodily performance, leaving traces of possibilities and potentialities rather than one, essentialist, 'woman'.

As the needle and thread pass up and down, to and fro, between the fragments of cloth, so they mimic those that have gone before. They differ, however, in the minutest shifts and changes of tension, of position, of relationships with warp and weft. Thus like the repeated mimicry by woman of herself, the one stitch and the many bring together fragments, fragments without a linear narrative between them, to form a matrix of knowledge that can be traversed in multiple ways. Each nomadic journey of writing in turn mimics those that went before, while simultaneously creating its own trajectories and its own linguistic performance.

Both writing and seaming, then, return their performance to the nomadic body, not as a passive palimpsest to be written upon, shaped and determined by circumstance, context and passage through the world, but rather as an active body that functions and performs conversationally within and between those forces, environments and passages as it travels. Thus, as the thread is drawn to and fro between the fabric pieces in the performance of seaming, the trace of its passage remains not only on the substrate, the cloth, but also on the thread itself: in its rubbed or softened edges. Both thread and fabric, joiner and joined, take on co-active roles in the production of the seam and meaning. Thread and fabric are active forces on each other that continuously and repeatedly reply and respond, even answer back.

In this there is the re-uttering and re-exploration of Sara Ahmed's concern for an approach which 'refuses to privilege mind over body' but 'emphasises contingency, locatedness, the irreducibility of difference . . . and the worldliness of being' (Ahmed 2001: 3). Such a phenomenological approach is one in which specifically located, individual experiences are the experiences through which that body relates to the world and other bodies. Each experience marks its trace and is marked simultaneously. Ahmed refers to this in terms of the 'with' of bodily relationship, or 'the fleshiness of the world which inhabits us and is inhabited by us' (2001: 5). To think then of seaming as trace is to think of it as Ahmed's 'with' or 'fleshiness'. Seaming opens the cloth to the thread, while simultaneously opening the thread to the cloth: separation becoming undermined in the intimate and proximate performance of the seaming.

Writing on stigmata, Cixous thinks not only of the marks, the constantly reopening wounds in sight, but also about how they came to be:

> Stigmata are traces of a sting. *Piquer* in French, to prick, to sting, to pinch, pricks in order to take, in order to prick, *piquer* steals, strikes and removes, sows, speckles signs it blows, leaves behind and takes away, annoys and excites at the same time, gives back what it takes, serves the interests of the thief and the police.
>
> (CIXOUS 1998: XIII)

In this passage Cixous sets out the basis for a collection of texts that she describes as having been 'stitched together sewn and resewn'(xi), suggesting a form of writing or making of the text that is about creating traces between, across and back, foregrounding 'with' in bodily relationship and a marking of those traces in the very fabric of those/that text. To think of seaming in terms of *piquer* or stinging is to think of a needle piercing the cloth and drawing through its surface the resistant thread: leaving behind the space of its passage, taking away the uniformity of the woven cloth. That piercing needle, that dragged thread, that pierced cloth – together bringing forth new possibilities, new paths to track, new avenues and new meanings to be brought into being.

Walter Benjamin, in his essay *The Storyteller* (1936), highlights such a form of narration that has its roots primarily in oral and experiential traditions and from which emerge or sprout multiple variants. He suggests that there are two kinds of storyteller: the traveller and the resident craftsperson, both of whom tell and retell the same stories (363). The storyteller's craft is to take experience, personal or received, and turn it into the experience of the audience. The traveller brings stories and variations from journeys taken while the craftsperson intricately embellishes these variations onto a personalized 'story-fabric' little by little. In this together they create a patchwork of conjoined and rejoined experiences, marking traces of journeys taken, imagined and proposed. Here the storytellers become needle and thread: pricking and stinging, leaving the irreducible marks of their presence.

Seaming itself, that performative act of fragment joining and being joined through piercings, threadings and stitching, could be thought of in terms of a materialization of such storytelling. For Benjamin 'storytelling is always the art of repeating stories' (367), but each seaming or performance of the story embeds itself differently within the listener – it becomes assimilated into and alongside other stories or other versions of the same story.

Thus the 'story-fabric' is brought into being through its own performance, a performance that, following Benjamin, relies heavily on a continued dynamic of agency between storyteller and listener: 'A man listening to a story is in the company of the storyteller; even a man reading one shares this companionship' (1936: 72). It is this companionship, with its prefix *com*, its withness and togetherness that create the story-fabric through a seaming together. Here is Showalter's multicentred patchwork quilt, joined in its non-hierarchy. The story-fabric is not built through linear narrative, which conventionally is structured around a beginning, a middle and endpoint that brings the recipient to a given point of destination. Rather this form has multiple centres, multiple routes through, and each journey upon the story-fabric emerges with differing and multiple points of focus.

Each nomadic journey is a series of new seamings of parts and fragments, in new arrangements: needle and thread each operating as both storyteller and listener, passing to and fro between the pieces, leaving traces of their performance in their wake. These traces become points of encounter on subsequent journeys or returns.

Italo Calvino, in his preface to *The Path to the Spiders' Nests* (1947) writes of Ariosto's epic poem *Orlando furioso* (1516) that it is:

> a book of landscapes, of rapidly sketched but vibrant figures, a book of words both precise and true.
>
> It is also an absurd, mysterious book, in which the object of pursuit is only pursued in order to pursue something else, and this something else is in turn pursued for the sake of something else again, and we never reach the ultimate goal.
>
> (CALVINO 1947: 27–8)

In this Calvino champions a form of writing, based upon the poetic and metaphoric, that operates as a story–fabric in much the same way as Benjamin's storyteller and Showalter's patchwork quilt, but in this preface he is concerned to highlight the agency that draws the fragments together, through memory, 'or rather experience – which is the memory of the event plus the wound it has inflicted on you, plus the change it has wrought in you' (Calvino 1947: 29). Such a seaming together of the different facets that form the basis for writing from the body suggests a mode of writing that could be considered to be an activity of dialogue or conversation between writer and readers rather than an act of communicating a given experience of the writer, by the writer for the reader to understand the writer's experience. Thinking of writing-as-seaming the story-fabric brings about a return to Cixous' *piquer* or sting, a way of making expression that builds upon retracings, refinding traces of previous journeys and sites of previous seamings. Like the stigmata, it is always open and reopening. This is a form of language construction that does not conceive of itself through being bounded or constrained by conventions, but rather it is enabled to burst out from within itself: writer and reader in dialogic or seaming relationship upon and within the story-fabric, an ever-expanding field of experience, imagination and mimicry.

To think of writing from the body as a mode for making expression that is a seaming, establishes it as part of the realm of bodily labour, perhaps even quotidian labour. In *The Red Dress* (2009–19) (Plates 11 and 12), Kirstie Macleod takes the practice of fine hand embroidery as a focus for such a story-fabric. In this work the embroiderer sits or stands, wearing a multilayered red silk dress, stitching and embellishing publicly. In this travelling, active, growing work, the dress crosses the globe, taking in 148 embroiderers from 28 countries, with each different addition there is a set of unique occasions, and the numbers are still growing. Artisans to date include refugees in Palestine, victims of civil war in Kosovo, Rwanda and DR Congo, individuals in South Africa, Kenya, Japan, Paris, Sweden, Colombia and Peru, upmarket studios in Bombay and Saudi Arabia alongside initiatives to support women in poverty such as Missibaba in Cape Town, South Africa, and Fanasina who work with Bedouin embroiderers based in the mountains above St Catherine's in Egypt's Sinai.

As it makes its journey, Macleod's dress moves physically between geographical locations, leaving traces of its presence in the photos, documentation and memories of those who stitched and wore it, alongside those who viewed it in its making. At the same time the dress carries physical evidence of its journeying between places and people on its surface. In this sense, the dress becomes as needle and thread, creating a new story-fabric with each passing, seaming together the different and unique events of its making to create a larger whole.

Claire Bishop, in her text on participation as a social and socializing form of production, suggests that such a social dimension, with its emphasis upon collaborative and collective approaches to art-making, sets such work as a departure from performance (2005: 10). According to Bishop's analysis, the participatory impulse continues to look to an active subject, to the ceding of authorial control and to collective responsibility, thus establishing a triadic structure of production: activation, authorship, community (12).

Bishop's concept of the social as a form of production, here in the guise of geographically separated seamstresses and travelling dress, can be considered in terms of the ephemeral gift: a seaming together of fragments across geographical, cultural and social divides. Here originality and authorship are challenged as ideas by which to conceive the works presented. Foster warns against what he perceives to be the danger of 'a promiscuity of collaborations' (Bishop 2006: 190–4) and the associated risk of illegibility that threatens to undermine the discursive and collaborative project.

Like the seamed and stitched garment that lies beneath the embroidery, *The Red Dress* operates as a signifier of its own topographical transformation: from Smith's flat paper pattern marked with its seam allowances, through to the red multilayered silk dress, through to its stitched and embellished surface, and further to its proposed free-standing sculptural form upheld by its own construction.

In *The Red Dress* Macleod locates the work of the seamstress as storyteller: intimately connected to the public activities of displaying or performing art, its publicity being vital to its legibility within culture. She positions her work at the interstice between public and private realms: the actions and activities of travelling and stitching operating as the points of articulation or seaming mechanisms between pieces and geographical locations. However, the work, in revealing the usually private act of making, disrupts and disturbs the public, drawing attention to its own purpose in the process, and potentially undermining it. Such repeated actions and activities, once established publicly as a visible part of art-making, seam together quotidian labour and artistic gesture. In this Macleod challenges the hierarchies and narratives associated with the privileging of certain practices over others, here specifically the work of the seamstress. This opens up a space in which place becomes possible, a space that borrows from, but does not become, gestation. In her seaming together of the multiple labours of art-making, Macleod performs Irigaray's reconceptualization of space and time:

> In order to make it possible to think through and live [sexual] difference, we must reconsider the whole problematic of space and time. . . . The transitions to a new age requires a change in our perception and conception of space–time, the inhabiting of places and of containers, or envelopes of identity.
> (IRIGARAY 1993: 8–9)

As *The Red Dress* travels between communities, it alters the way in which that performance's own production is perceived and framed. As such it foregrounds the trace of the artwork's production as needle and thread passing to and fro, back and forth, between the pieces of cloth in the construction of the seam. Initially the work sought to generate a dialogue of identity through embroidery, and a merging of cultural boundaries and borders, but over the years as it collected stories of all involved the dress has taken on its own agency. It has managed to travel and access disparate communities worldwide, being given entry directly into the skilled hands of some of the world's vulnerable people: victims of war and oppression who are often not given a voice and are among the poorest in the world in monetary terms.

In this sense, then, Macleod brings to the fore both the hidden seam allowance and the reverse of the seamed cloth, championing structural elements and their characteristics as vital and necessary aspects of the agency that draws the fragments together. Here Cixous' *piquer* and Benjamin's 'story-fabric' come together as a means of making meaning built upon retracings and refinding of traces of previous journeys, performances, maintenance activities and sites of previous seamings.

Conjunctions and crossings

This chapter reflects upon and considers ways and means by which knowledge gained through the intimate technologies tied up with making seams can be expressed through those practices, processes and technologies. In this, seaming has been considered as both a physical process and as a concept through which to think of a pathway between theoretical and practice-based concerns.

In thinking through and with seaming as a model for conjoining or bringing together differing elements, the physical and necessarily bodily technologies of hand-stitching have been foregrounded. The three aspects of this: seaming as passage, seaming as suturing and seaming as trace offer different, but associated modes for this reflection. Seaming as passage focuses upon the shared space of making and writing which prioritizes to-ing and fro-ing between as a structure for understanding. This is an intimate space of coming-into-being or perhaps coming-into-understanding, where tacit and explicit language mingle and the semiotic chora is recovered. Seaming as suturing, by contrast, offers a way for thinking through and with the thickened space. This is a speaking-space that defies narrative and chronologically constrained forms of writing in favour of multiplicity. Here, between tacit and explicit knowledge and language, meaning is oblique, multiple, mutable and partial, a tactic adopted to enable occupation of Cixous' 'scarry' habitat.

Operating as a triangulation of the concept of seaming, seaming as trace suggests a mode for meditation upon the technologies of seaming, through which the potentiality and multiplicity of outcomes are opened up. Seaming as trace places the focus of joining and conjoining as nomadic mappings and journeyings. With each new departure across the 'story–fabric' comes a new performance in which there is a continued dynamic of agency between path, ground, writer–maker and viewer–reader.

In creating 'new' fabric, seaming brings together the agency of maker, writer, reader and viewer, foregrounding the bodily activities or technologies of stitching that both heal and celebrate Cixous' *piquer*. In this, then, the seam and seaming as an activity suggests a form of language construction that does not conceive of itself through being bounded or constrained by conventions, but rather it is enabled to burst out from within itself: writer and reader in dialogic or seaming relationship upon and within the story-fabric, an ever-expanding field of experience, imagination and mimicry.

4
TEXTILE AS VISCOUS SUBSTANCE

In general terms, and drawing upon the word's etymology, a viscous substance is a substance or material with a thick, sticky consistency somewhere between a solid and a liquid. That substance's viscosity is an active function of a substance's structure and is measured in terms of that stickiness or clinging-ness through testing its resistance to external pressures.

To think of textile as a viscous substance is, firstly, to focus upon its ability to take up both solid and liquid-like properties and, secondly, to consider its stickiness or its tendency to cling not only physically to the body but also metaphorically in the form of textile words and meanings. Taken together, these modes of approaching textile in terms of a viscous substance refer to one another: textile and language, liquid and solid. It is a referential relationship based upon clinging-ness or stickiness, one in which they melt and flow towards each other.

In this sense this chapter proposes woven cloth as a space for thinking through the interplay of textile's structure and its behaviour. The intimate relationship between warp and weft directs the behaviour of the resultant cloth. Reciprocally, the required behaviour of the woven cloth dictates the selected warp–weft relationship. Behaviour and structure flow in and around one another. For example, silk satin is particularly favoured for wedding dresses, evening gowns and lingerie because of its lustre and draping properties, which are a direct result of its structure. In plain weave, alternate warp threads are raised, the weft thread is passed between the two sets of threads and then the system is reversed so that those that were raised are lowered and those that were beneath are raised, resulting in the familiar under-over-under-over pattern. In satin weave it is every fifth warp thread that is raised, the weft passed between, and the whole pattern is shifted along by one thread, resulting in a large number of 'floating' weft threads, which give the cloth its sheen or lustre. The drape is achieved through the choice of threads in combination with this weave pattern, resulting in a cloth that appears to flow over any substrate.

Consider muslin: woven from inexpensive, unbleached white cotton and used for a variety of uses, such as clothing in hot dry climates, straining liquids and pulps for culinary purposes and dressings for medical purposes. Woven loosely and using the same carded cotton fibres for warp and weft, muslin cloth is primarily a cheap cloth to manufacture, highly absorbent and its loose weave allows air to move easily through it, thus rendering it highly useful in a wide range of situations. Again, structure and behaviour are inextricably linked together.

In her essay, 'Contemporary Textiles: the art fabric' (in Monem 2008: 32–61), Janis Jefferies expands and dissects the notion of what the textile is and might be, suggesting that fabric, cloth and fibres operate within the realm of the metaphor, enabling words and things, fibre and material to interweave one another. Jefferies presents a space for cloth's materiality that acts as a springboard for thinking, thinking that draws on cloth's utilitarian and ubiquitous presence alongside cultural power for expression.

Jefferies' model for thinking about cloth is particularly useful here in that she establishes textile as a medium that is naturally deconstructive, that is at once sensorially and philosophically charged with critical language. To think of woven cloth is to think of warp, weft and fibres together and separately, but always in relationship with one another. It is from here that this chapter sets out, firstly turning to useful philosophical framings of the viscous to unpack its usefulness as a metaphor before then turning back to cloth and artists working with cloth in ways that reveal cloth and that which makes cloth as viscous, sticky substance. The artists and artworks featured are Chiharu Shiota, who spins webs that engulf and entrap; Rosalind Wyatt, whose stitched calligraphy materializes the fluidity of ink in thread; and the oozing sculptural forms of Julie René de Cotret and Elinor Whidden. While working in distinctly different ways and with differing points of departure, what brings these artists together here is a foregrounding of the potency of cloth as a substance that is at once fluid and solid, sticky and clinging.

As a philosophical concept, the viscous has been drawn upon by Jean-Paul Sartre, who considered the notion of viscosity to be a phenomenon that is

> neither material (and physical) nor psychic, about which transcends the opposition of the psychic and the physical by revealing itself as an ontological expression of the world as a whole.
>
> (SARTRE 1943: 627)

In suggesting that viscosity transcends the opposition of mind and body, Sartre proposes an *a priori* link between the two poles within the viscous relationship and as such establishes a relationship between them which foregrounds thickness and stickiness, a relationship based on clinging-ness.

The material clinging-ness or stickiness between the two states within the viscous provokes a sense of horror for Sartre (1943: 626), something echoed by Julia Kristeva in her account of abjection, in which she describes her gag response to the viscous, slimy skin on the surface of cooled milk (Kristeva 1982: 79), and to which I will return within this chapter. For others there are what could be considered more productive contexts of viscous substances, mostly drawing on their ability to lubricate, but the productive potential encompasses the oozing, sweetness of honey and the sensuous silkiness of molten chocolate. Viscous substances are at their most potent at the boundaries of the body: on its skin and at its orifices, seducing and repelling. Taken as a viscous substance, cloth's potency for creating expression lies in its interplay with the body, its slippage against the skin that creates extra-bodily sensorial spaces.

For the purposes here, the viscous will be considered in terms of its potential as a metaphor by which to consider cloth and body in mixture and flow as a mode for the interplay between textile practice and theory. The stickiness towards one another creates a potent space of exchange. The stickiness between solid and liquid will be taken as a key theme here, particularly through the writings of Julia Kristeva and social anthropologist Mary Douglas. These are important here in that they address Sartre's abhorrence of all that is sticky or viscous, allowing for a rehabilitation of the term.

Kristeva's notion of the abject and abjection presents a mode of feminist thinking that transcends bodily boundaries between outside and inside, establishing the idea of in-between substances or an alternative symbolic order in which subject–object distinctions collapse and signifier–signified relationships become disturbed. Douglas, in her critique of Sartre's viscosity, further develops the idea of stickiness between states by drawing attention to similarities between such substances and one's own secretions:

> The viscous is a state halfway between solid and liquid. It is like a cross-section in a process of change. It is unstable but it does not flow. It is soft, yielding and compressible. There is no gliding on its surface. Its stickiness is a trap, it clings like a leech; it attacks the boundary between myself and it. Long columns falling off my fingers suggest my own substance flowing into the pool of stickiness.
>
> (DOUGLAS 1966: 38)

Both Kristeva and Douglas open out the notion of the viscous to consider woman's relationship with herself and the medium for doing so: mucous. Irigaray goes further and identifies this as one of the foremost substances that differentiates the masculine world from that of women (Irigaray 1984: 18), establishing it as a mode for considering a subjectivity in which the solid and the visible are displaced by the viscous and the felt: a mucous-subjectivity experienced from within. Mucous becomes a mediating substance, or what Hilary Robinson refers to as a 'morphology of the mucous' (Robinson 2006: 104).

All of these approaches focus upon the 'halfway between' nature of viscous substances and the concept of the viscous as a process of change, or passage, between states, which further emphasizes the tension between solid and liquid. This chapter suggests a model for textile practice–theory expression in which each is actively recognized and present in the other. This (inter)relationship suggests that the engagement between them is active, clinging, yielding and thus unstable in nature. Returning to Sartre, the viscous substance offers a reading of cloth that is built upon an ontological[2] mode of expression, a means for thinking through the relationships that exist between textile structure, its behaviour and the body across which it moves.

Returning to silk satin and cotton muslin highlights the broader fact that the relationship between structure and behaviour is at the very heart of the textile. This interplay lends itself to be drawn upon to mirror the structure and behaviour of the viscous substance in which the relationship between the different molecules within that substance dictates its level of resistance to external pressure. The closer and more electrically attracted to each other the molecules are, the higher the resistance to external stresses, the weaker the electrical attraction then the lower the resistance. Moreover, as viscous substances have the potential to simultaneously symbolize sensuousness and the abject, erotic attraction and repulsion, so too does the woven cloth hold its own sets of simultaneous contradictions: concealing–revealing (the body), active–passive, constriction–revelation. These contradictions cling to each other, holding cloth in active flow – neither fully liquid, nor fully solid, but a cross-section in a process of change.

In this chapter, structures and behaviours of cloth will be considered together with the concept of the viscous to consider ways in which they can be drawn upon within textile practices as a model of practice–theory (inter)relationships. Cloth, like Sartre's 'slimy', Douglas' long columns falling off her fingers and Irigaray's 'mucous', holds neither the 'reassuring inertia of the solid' nor the 'dynamism like that in water' (Sartre 1943: 630). Rather it clings and sucks, flows and falls, its substance threatening to engulf and dissolve the boundaries.

The artists and artworks that are drawn upon within this chapter include Rosalind Wyatt, Julie René de Cotret and Elinor Whidden and Chiharu Shiota, each selected to consider the usefulness and validity of viscosity as a model for textile practice–theory (inter)relationships. To this end Wyatt's *The Stitch Lives of London* (2011–) highlights viscous bodily metaphors and activities as she moves between flowing ink, handwritten texts, stitch, thread and cloth, focusing on handwritten texts rendered in stitch to mark the boundary between interior and exterior (of the body); de Cotret and Whidden's collaborative residency at VSVSVS (Ontario, Canada 2013) references lives lived, through upholstered forms and reconfigured furniture: overstuffed and oozing from themselves, the sculptures address the viscous through comfort and excess; Chiharu Shiota spins woollen webs and cocoons in *After the Dream* (2009–11), creating a vertiginous space where subject and object, interior and exterior, self and other are brought together at a site of viscous production. To return to Barthes' drawing together of text and tissue, these artists demonstrate, through their practice, different aspects of his hyphology: their work is generated 'in a perpetual interweaving' (Barthes 1973: 64), the subject, here textile, repeatedly making and unmaking itself in the process.

Attacking the boundary

The mouth is interesting because it is one of those places where the dry outside moves towards the slippery inside.
(ARTIST JENNY HOLZER, *The living series,* 1989)

In this statement Jenny Holzer draws attention not only to the passage between inside and outside of the body and the change of state that such a transition requires but also to the movement and flow of saliva that marks it. Focusing upon such transitions and movement between states complicates and extends subject–object relationships into the realm of viscosity and viscous substances a 'in-between' or liminal substances. Considered through a feminist approach in which binary subject–object relationships are collapsed, opens out a space that enables subject–subject or self–same relationships, a space in which woman's relationship with herself can be considered. Luce Irigaray identifies the medium for this relationship as mucous (Irigaray 1984: 304). The woman inhabits a world of moist mucous-ness, a secretion and accretion-based existence. Mucous, as woman's secretion, becomes a mode of subjectivity I will refer to as mucous–subjectivity, that complicates boundaries as it is secreted.

In *An Ethics of Sexual Difference* (1984) Irigaray sets out the ground for such mucous-subjectivity in terms of the role of mucous as a mediating substance for any thinking from the female (304). Such a mode also establishes a model for subjectivity that shifts the focus from notions of truth, solidity and stability to those which foreground slipperiness and instability and with them notions of subjectivity as production and generation that echo the processual and resistant nature of the viscous.

Feminist theorist Hilary Robinson suggests such a mode of thinking presents a 'morphology of the mucous' (Robinson 2006: 98), a classification that highlights the role of mucous within and between woman–woman and woman–man relationships, but also woman–herself relations. In this sense, then, thinking through mucous focuses upon, and questions, the status of the boundaries of the female body: 'the very openness of their bodies, of their flesh, of their genitals makes the question of boundaries difficult' (Irigaray 1984: 43). Robinson, through her analysis of Irigaray's writing, explores the idea that a mucous-based subjectivity is concerned with porous boundaries, viscosity, flow and production. Mucous-subjectivity does not follow the rules of the solid, within which the molecules are held together in fixed regimes. Rather, what is proposed is a subjectivity whose molecules are held together more loosely and thus can shift and slide alongside and in mixture with neighbouring substances or other subjects, they cling and stick to each other.

Such secretions and accretions at the boundaries of bodies have been taken up by a number of, mainly female, artists, often in the guise of other, similarly viscous substances that cross Holzer's boundary between dry and wet. These substances circumscribe bodies often through cultural location and becoming transgressive in that resistance. Such tensions result in harmless activities being taken up as a strategic, metaphoric and powerful tool for artists to explore and express bodily themes.

Rosalind Wyatt works with ink, brush, pen, needle and thread in her series *The Stitch Lives of London* (2011–date) to tell the stories and lives of historical and contemporary characters. As her ink meets paper it hangs between pen (or brush) and the surface, before sinking into it. In an echo of this, her needle draws her thread through the cloth, bringing it to the surface where it hovers between surface and substance. Like the River Thames, Wyatt's texts, penned and stitched, flow across the paper/cloth. Like the stories of the Londoners that are Wyatt's subjects, thread and ink cling to the surface, hovering between flowing liquid and static solid forms. They cling and yet at the same time flow from those surfaces.

Wyatt works between handwritten texts, stitch and cloth, drawing the stories of her characters together. One particularly powerful item within the series is a cotton running singlet entitled *A Boy Who Loved to Run* (Plate 13). At first unnoteworthy, a ubiquitous men's vest of the early 1990s. On the reverse, however, Wyatt has meticulously stitched the final, and unfinished, school essay of Stephen Lawrence (Plate 14). Her skill as a calligrapher, her ability to follow the movements of his pen and ink on paper, through stitch and cloth, gives the text back its fluidity, together with Lawrence's stumbles, pauses and crossings out; Lawrence left the essay mid-sentence. Stitch, thread and text cling to the surface of his running vest, drawing the reader into the essay, all the while recognizing the broader narratives of a young black man needlessly killed by a gang of white youths in 1993, a mother mourning and the cultural rupture that ensued and continues in the wake of this young man. As Wyatt says of this piece, 'It will not flinch from showing the conflicts of the past and present, alongside the comic, the wonderful, the strange and the beautiful' (interview with Wyatt, June 2016).

This is Lawrence's running vest, complete with its bobbled surface, the worn away label, its faded trimming particularly noticeable at the underarms. Lawrence loved to run, he loved sports and he won medals for his achievements.

He sweated and this sweat crossed the boundary of his skin onto the vest, much as Wyatt's stitches and Lawrence's writing penetrate the cloth again. As the body moves and sweats, text flows onto the paper, sweat onto cloth and in Wyatt's hands the vest becomes a viscous substance, held between liquid and solid in the process of change, absorbing bodily fluids in viscous exchange.

To return to Mary Douglas' description of the viscous is to dwell with a reading in which the everyday activities of sweating, consumption, sexual intercourse and childbirth, bleeding, menstruation and death are brought together as viscous, mucous-bound bodily activities and processes at its boundaries and on its surfaces. Life is encountered through the viscous. This is Douglas' 'cross-section in a process of change' between body and non-body, establishing the relationship between states within the viscous at the boundaries of the body materially and conceptually.

In *The Stitch Lives of London*, polarities could be said to be brought into a relationship, which foreground the thickness and stickiness of the viscous and mucous in particular: between soft and hard, self and other, male and female, black and white. In Wyatt's work pleasure and devastation, care and abject horror mingle: the vest becomes in excess of itself, seemingly unable to contain its own ubiquity. Janis Jefferies notes that 'The softness and ultimate fragility of cloth are linked to organic bodily matter and the vulnerability of humans, whose every relationship is transient, subject to the degenerative process of decay and death' (Jefferies in Livingstone and Ploof 2007: 284). *A Boy Who Loved to Run*, like the other works in Wyatt's *London Lives* series, addresses the body's margins, its edgy, unwanted spaces of frayage. Lawrence's vest acknowledges sweat and death, loss and vulnerability, aspects of the abject that offer a passage through which to explore the pleasures, horrors and dangers of the body's limits through its viscosity.

Jenni Sorkin speaks of cloth's ability to hold the 'sometimes unbearable gift of memory' (2000: 77) and suggests that stains or marks on fabric destroy the continuity of the cloth physically, culturally and metaphorically. Stains elicit shame and cross the boundaries of good behaviour. What Wyatt's work does is to address the notion of the stain, but with ink and writing telling its own story, reasserting itself and rupturing that which has gone before at the surface of the cloth. Her texts tell stories of hardship, mourning, degradation and fear, but in reuniting handwriting, clothing and content, these stories take on new meaning. Through Wyatt's stains, Sorkin's present-past is realized and in the discontinuity of the cloth memory is released.

Collapsing boundaries

In discussing the transgression of the bodily boundary Kristeva's construct of the abject becomes a key point of interest. When faced with an abject object or experience, she suggests that a sudden psychological reaction is provoked in which there is a confusion of self with other, subject with object, such that 'meaning collapses' at the borderline (Kristeva 1982: 2). In this she identifies three main types of 'in-between' substance (4): food, excrement and the feminine/maternal body. Abjection is caused by that which

> disturbs identity, system, order. What does not respect borders, positions, rules. The in-between, the ambiguous, the composite.
>
> (KRISTEVA 1982: 4)

In crossing bodily boundaries, the abject threatens to collapse subject–object distinctions, resulting in irrational responses such as that Kristeva herself experiences at the sight of the skin on the surface of cooled milk: 'a gagging sensation and, still further down, spasms in the stomach, the belly' (Kristeva 1982: 79). As the boundaries collapse, so Kristeva's theory suggests, it is as if 'death [is]infecting life . . . it beckons to us and ends up engulfing us' (4). The abject fascinates desire and it is in the push–pull, subject–object confusion or diffusion that meaning collapses and all that is left is a pre-verbal, non-linguistic sense at the very borderlines of the self, a form of excess of itself, which could be said to parallel Sartre's viscous and offers within the abject a space for mucous-subjectivity.

In the seemingly boundary-less space between internal and external, between Holzer's 'dry' outside and 'slippery' inside, mucous is secreted, creating a space of slippage that both literally and metaphorically collapses oppositional structures. As the site is traversed so a process of transformation could be said to occur: food taken into the body via the mouth enters as one form of organic matter and then, as a result of bodily actions, becomes sweat, urine, blood and faeces.

These viscous substances are held within the fibres, the story and the stitched text of Lawrence's vest. Categorization between inside and outside of the body is challenged and denied. In the destabilized state between solid and liquid Wyatt emulates the rhythm and spontaneity of Lawrence's handwriting, his unique mark left behind, clinging onto the cloth like a stain, through her hand. Wyatt's work is concerned with words, their sound and feel, articulated in ways that bring into focus the intimate relationship between cloth and skin. The words cling to the cloth, continuing and maintaining Lawrence's presence and affect within the world.

In interview, Wyatt speaks of her response to words and handwritten text as a 'voice'. In this she blurs the boundaries that define self–other ontological structuring of the world. In her work the bodily actions, activities and productions of the artist and subject come together through associations and visceral interactions, her stitched threads clinging to the surface of the cloth as the ink in the moments between liquid held in the pen and solid pigment in the page. The stitched words intrude into the garment, not to disrupt and degrade, but to complete and to rehabilitate the relationship between cloth and body (interview with Wyatt, June 2016).

Flow

According to Sartre, viscosity is neither material nor psychic, but a phenomenon which transcends such terms, emerging instead as an ontological expression of the world as a whole (Sartre 1943: 627). On first encountering de Cotret and Whidden's collaborative structures there is a strange sense of bodily recognition. This is evidently furniture that has been deconstructed, reconstructed, dismantled and forensically examined. And yet, it is in fact all about us. About how we are incarnated as bodies. In many ways one of the most striking aspects of this work is that it is instantly recognizable as about one's body and at the same time instantly recognizable as overstuffed, uptight formal furniture. The furniture was originally built in Newmarket, Ontario, in the 1960s, but in the collaboration between de Cotret and Whidden at VSVSVS (2013) the three-piece suite has undergone a series of procedures that are investigative, exploratory and intrusive. Through these procedures the work explores the relationship between Canada's manufacturing boom, the moment in which the furniture was built, and today's neoliberal, late capitalist context which is the result of the global boom and mass production of such goods. The work questions and challenges often unspoken notions of excess, comfort and decadence.

The sculptures are playful and their reconfigurations amuse and delight as they ooze and overspill their upholstered bindings. They have been plundered and undergone internal reorganization. The work slips into the spaces between domestic and public, sculpture and manufacture, excess and exorbitance, creative expression and fly-tipped detritus. The work becomes Sartre's notion of the viscous as ontological expression. The reimagined three-piece suite does not represent, it *is*.

While this work could be a simple commentary, even moral judgement, upon the inevitable aftermath of a period of excess and decadence, it doesn't stop there. From within the reconstructed and reconfigured furniture emerges an ambivalence of this excess. With its feet now facing outwards rather than demurely supporting, and with the space where one would once have sat neatly now bloated and straining against its own buttons, in its soft tactile and transient materiality, the larger sofa evokes the rhythms, actions and mortality of the bodies that made, used and discarded it.

In reintroducing the body to the manufactured product, de Cotret and Whidden's collaborations create a realm of parallel objects that extend and contract their ubiquity and recognizability. In their excess and surplus, they challenge cycles of production, consumption and disposal, and expose the logic of a value-based economy.

As these works offer their critique of the economy of production, they expose a space of nothingness that problematizes its own existence. This space of nothingness, read through de Cotret and Whidden's oozing, burgeoning forms, attacks its own boundaries, it opens its body to reveal its mucous-subjectivity.

The VSVSVS collaboration has its origins in furniture production, the ready-made and the surreal, mirroring its own visual viscosity. The works unravel the terms of reference for the viewer's interaction with the sculptural surfaces and space it articulates. Held taut by the upholstery techniques, the work threatens to break its bounds and ooze and flow away from its frame. The work is provisional and contingent, caught as if in the process of change, sticking and clinging to its frames and form, neither fully liquid not fully solid.

The forms, then, draw the viewer into the viscosity of the raw materials and processes of construction, to the ways in which each layer of stuffing and covering pulls and clings to the previous layer, rendering the interplay between them a site of active engagement. This adds to the work's palpability. The displaced legs and reorganized structures reveal the layers of dense wadding, buttoning and coverings that result in this oozing, yielding, burgeoning form. It mimics the fleshly body.

In one of the pieces in de Cotret and Whidden's collection, the splayed covering of an armchair is strapped within an irregular wooden frame like an animal's pelt. Held thus, the work becomes more than surface or covering, drawing attention to the matter, the structure and form of the chair from which it came. Structure and form are held in tension, pulling and stretching at each other.

The viewer tries to reconstruct where the arms, legs, back and seat of the chair once were through the traces and marks left. In so doing, the 'missing' internal workings of the chair become present in their absence. The form takes on an unstable and transitory mode, the surfaces unresolved and in a state of flux or flow. They cling to their origin in the chair and their newly splayed location renders them suspended between solid and liquid, self and other, interior and exterior.

De Cotret and Whidden take the notion of discarded furniture, with its previous existence and occupants, as a means by which to offer scope for thinking between textile practice and thinking in terms of the viscous. As the fabrics and stuffing are pulled, stretched, restuffed and reconfigured, they cling to their older selves, while oozing away to disintegration. Marion Milner writes of such an embodied encounter with materials (Milner 1950), which suggests an interplay between conscious and unconscious modes of thinking. In terms of textile practice and theory, de Cotret and Whidden's re-crafting of used furniture draws attention to their materials, but also the processes those materials have undergone both in the making and through the re-use. Claire Pajaczkowska notes:

> The practice of making textiles holds, tends and carries something of the undisciplined, because it is multi- and inter-disciplinary, and also something of the dangerously collaborative and relational.
> (PAJACZKOWSKA IN JEFFERIES ET AL 2016: 83)

This is the crux of de Cotret and Whidden's work and why they present an important point of focus here. In the embodied encounter with the furniture of VSVSVS, the practice of working with textiles and the theories surrounding these practices are held in active and viscous tension.

Ontological secretions

Where de Cotret and Whidden present the viewer with oozing, escaping forms, the work of Japanese artist Chiharu Shiota threatens entrapment within dense webs of threads. Shiota's *hyphology* entails themes of remembrance, home and the loss of childhood and result in the production of mysterious, disturbing and often frightening art works. As the spider, Shiota spins her webs, her tissue, to incorporate and engulf her prey, which are sometimes chairs, pianos, beds, dresses, flights of stairs or found ephemera of life. These thread secretions or installations literally invade the space[1], establishing a tensional field which captures and involves the viewer at the boundary between the familiar and the unfamiliar, safety and danger. While threatening to entrap, the works also suggest a place of refuge both within the threads, but also within the beds, under the skirts of the dresses, in the absent cupboard under the stairs. In these web works, Shiota materializes an ontological expression which brings together mind and body in Sartrean viscous relationship:

> I am. I am, I exist, therefore I am; I am because I think that I don't want to be, I think that . . . because . . . ugh! I flee.
> (SARTRE 1938: 137)

In this Sartre and Shiota come together, foregrounding the tensional and sticky interplay between repulsion and attraction as modelled by the viscous. Both fleeing and creating Barthes' constructive secretions of the spider's web/tissue.

There is a Japanese legend, according to Shiota[2], in which an invisible red thread is attached at birth to the little finger which connects to one's future life partner – it may tangle or stretch, but never break. Life with death is a recurrent theme in Shiota's work and the matrix of threads echoes both this legend but also references the umbilical cord that joins mother and child. These are sticky themes, which in relationship with one another, foreground the viscosity of their intertwining: life inevitably becomes entangled with death, but the beginning and end are neither seen nor known fully. Instead, in the viscosity of living, both beginning and end cling to each other like Douglas's substance falling off her fingers.

Such ideas are particularly highlighted in Shiota's 2009 work, *After the Dream* (Plates 15 and 16), an installation created for the Hayward Gallery's 'Walking in My Mind' (2009) exhibition and subsequently installed in Galerie La Maison Rouge, Paris (2011) and the 'Lost in Lace' exhibition (2011–12) in Birmingham. In this Shiota extended her web to every wall of the gallery space, positioning in the very centre of this part-dream, part-nightmare scenario, five oversized dresses, hovering in a ring as if their absent owners were holding hands. The whole ensemble was held in suspended animation within the mass of web surrounding them. This work opens out to the viewer a psychic space for the unconscious (Shiota's and/or the viewer's), materializing the dream/nightmare. The dresses, uninhabited, operate as both subject and object, standing in for the absent artist/ performer and disorienting the viewer. Further, the elongated forms of the dresses produce a space within which the viewer is rendered an infant once more, standing at the mother's feet. Simultaneously, the dresses, behind their veil of cobwebs, are redolent with female polysemy: are they nightgowns, shrouds, wedding dresses, ball gowns – meaning is endlessly deferred, held within the viscosity of knowing/unknowing. The elongated skirts suggest the potential for a place of refuge, thus placing them on the borderline between refuge/engulfing – Kristeva's *chora* – a space of expressions that precede language and therefore a space which challenges linguistically chartered territory.

When shown at Galerie La Maison Rouge, Paris (March–May 2011), the dresses had moved on in their dance and now formed an orderly line, as if in promenade or awaiting some fate. This new arrangement changes the nature and quality of the web: where before the dresses seemed cocooned and potentially the source of the web, here it appeared more delicate and there was no hub of existence. In this Paris staging, the black threads felt less like secretions and somehow more oppressive within this delicacy. In this sense, then, the web structure itself moves between its liquid state at the point of secretion, to the fully dried state after the prey has been dissolved and devoured and the web abandoned. Do these dresses stand as secreting spider or prey awaiting capture and dissolution? Shown in the 'Lost in Lace' exhibition in Birmingham Museum and Art Gallery (October 2011–February 2012) as part of a mixed exhibition, the dresses were rearranged again. This time they stood in a semicircle as if holding hands in a game or communal dance. The artist installs these works in a direct response to the space and explained that in this venue, because the viewer could not walk all the way around the installation, the dresses were positioned in this manner to create a form of dialogue with the viewer.[3] Further, the concept behind Lesley Millar's curation of this exhibition focused upon the notion of lace as a permeable (visual, physical and metaphorical) boundary space. In this sense, then, the presentation of Shiota's dresses behind their semi-transparent fretwork or matrix of threads, offers the viewer both entrapment and freedom, claustrophobia and a lightness of presence, 'leading us into those areas of the mind where darkness illuminates recollected images' (Millar 2011: 11).

In Shiota's work, the ambivalence or simultaneity of meaning is held in viscous relationship like the dresses – between past and future, dream and reality, security and danger, solid and liquid. As in a nightmare sequence, insecurities from the past pose as anxieties for the future without ever fully referencing either temporal location, so too in Shiota's work, within the sticky mucous web of thread, does the viewer find themselves caught between and amidst this relational interplay.

In positioning Shiota's practice as a viscous form of art-making, I want to suggest that this operates beyond the relationship between liquid and solid. A model of viscosity offers flow and rates of flow, change and transformation between. It is a model that celebrates the visceral alongside and in mixture with the visual; it draws attention to the relationship and movement *between* states. Within Shiota's web works there is contained a sense of suspended animation, but further, a state of flux or the suspension of some form of transformative process. It is almost as if the spider's spinning of its web has been frozen in a moment of time, thus revealing Douglas's cross-section in a process of change.

In her book *Metamorphoses: towards a materialist theory of becoming* (2002) Rosi Braidotti suggests that the notion of transformation can be considered to be, or indeed renamed, 'becoming' and

> is the actualization of the immanent encounter between subjects, entities and forces which are apt mutually to affect and exchange parts of each other in a creative and non-invidious manner.
>
> (BRAIDOTTI 2002: 68)

These ideas, Braidotti notes, draw on Deleuze's 'radical immanence' that emphasizes connectivity over separation and difference. Thus 'becoming' prioritizes affectivity of the subject, while simultaneously emphasizing the temporal contextualization of the embodied subject. Becoming involves varying levels of affectivity between subjects, but also it is an unfolding form of transformation of possibilities, potentialities and alternatives. This activity cuts against and through dualisms and binarism in that it does not necessitate the 'either . . . or' decision, but rather enables the 'both . . . and' and thus is multiple and mutable – a plastic and elastic mode of transformation.

Thinking about Shiota's web works and specifically *After the Dream* in these terms offers ways in which (female) pleasure can be brought centre stage, not pleasure as bodily immersion in sensation, but through transformation of the viewing body's subjectivity into a broader frame of reference. This transformation suggests an opening up the body to a system of meaning beyond the limits of rationality and builds upon the practices of such influences on Shiota as her teacher and mentor Marina Abramovic together with, I would suggest, Carolee Schneemann, Rebecca Horn, Eva Hesse, Janine Antoni and Louise Bourgeois.

Shiota's work largely concerns the transformation of experiences, memories and recollections into sculptural processes and performance. In so doing, Shiota's webs draw subject to subject: viewers are cast as co-producers of meaning as they inhabit Shiota's space of productive transformation with all its plasticity, mutability and multiplicity. As the viewer is brought into proximal relationship with the viscous webs and their prey, so too does the bodily space of that sculptural process draw the viewer's body into that viscous mix.

A substance between two states

Nothing testifies more clearly to its ambiguous character as a 'substance between two states' than the slowness with which the slimy melts into itself.
(SARTRE 1943: 628)

As the viscous honey pours down onto viscous honey, self onto self, it is held separate temporarily before the resistance is overcome and its softness yields, enfolding and engulfing the new part. In establishing the viscous as a model for exploring ways in which cloth takes on different states both materially and metaphorically, it is this stickiness and slowness that have become key concerns. However, when the notion of cloth as viscous is brought into the model, not in terms of its structure but in terms of its behaviour (which of course is a corollary of its structure) and associated metaphorical language, cloth takes on a mucous-subjectivity that builds upon its inherently ambiguous self. In this, then, cloth becomes a means of expression from and of the body, rather than by the body, to use Cixous' description of *écriture fèminine*. It is a mode that is about cloth, with cloth and for cloth, all three in sticky mixture. In the work of Chiharu Shiota, her hyphology and web catch the viewers up in the web of threads, drawing them onto the surfaces of the dresses within the tensional field that destabilizes and confounds in its viscous, sticky web. Wyatt, by contrast, brings bodiliness and its secretions into being through ink, thread and cloth in her *Stitched Lives of London* series: here cloth and text cling to one another through the language, syntax and words that penetrate the surface. As Wyatt reconstructs the handwritten, unfinished essay of Stephen Lawrence, blood, sweat, tears and death, cling and stick together in mucous-filled exchange. Finally, de Cotret and Whidden's collaborative sculptural forms, ooze and threaten to spill outwards, like flesh held within too-tight clothes, they threaten to reveal that which is meant to be contained. They are transgressive and wild in their expression of cloth as an ambiguous substance. In these upholstered sculptures, cloth is both surface and form, held in a mucous, viscous space that is both embodied and disembodied simultaneously.

To think of cloth as viscous substance is to think of it in terms of its ability to intermingle and thus to actively challenge notions of visual 'truth' as a singular mode of expression. These installations are ways of seeing, knowing and looking towards a bodiliness at the same time as shifting touching, making and feeling towards a broader perceptual framework beyond the body through the cloth. Thus cloth, surface and form, in their stickiness towards each other, collapse together into viscous, flowing, oozing forms of mutually re-enforcing registers of expression. It could be said that in many ways they emphasize and celebrate the specificity and difference of each other. They flow and ooze together, measured in terms of their resistance to external pressure.

5
FRAYING

In his catalogue essay for the exhibition *TRA* in the Palazzo Fortuny, Venice as part of the 2011 Biennale, Axel Vervoordt unravels the title *TRA*, not only as the word ART reversed but further as a prefix and suffix that crosses cultural and linguistic divides. *Tra-* (along with *trans-*) as a prefix adds the notion of across, through and over (e.g. traverse, traduce and tradition), while *-tra* as a suffix changes the root word to the means of doing something (e.g. mantra becomes a means of thinking and tantra becomes a style of mediation that stretches or liberates). *TRA*, he suggests, can be thought of as 'a gateway between worlds' (2011: 3). As a threshold or borderline is crossed, so a new landscape is revealed: the edge of becoming. Vervoordt considers the exhibition as a journey, a proposal, with a focus upon the spaces and connections between. In curating this collection of artworks, he plays with the notion of the boundary or threshold and these spaces or gaps between. Building and exhibition seep and dissolve one into another, blurring the edges and highlighting connectivities.

In this sense Vervoordt offers an alternative spatiality that privileges the hiatus, intervention and plasticity and thus *TRA* offers a way for thinking about the threshold not as a passage between here and there, but rather a vertiginous place between the absolute and the void.

I would like to propose here that such a place can be modelled in terms of frayed and fraying woven cloth. To think of fraying cloth is to focus upon its construction being revealed: the edges fragmented, warp and weft slipping apart. This chapter considers the fragmented, frayed and holey, an approach that Gayatri Spivak refers to as 'spacy emptiness' (1993: 398). Drawing together Spivak, Derrida, Cixous and Haraway, I want to point to a mode of thinking through language and cloth that lies beyond syntax and weave, to consider a cross-cultural landscape that, like frayed cloth, is contingent and permanently in negotiation.

Julia Bryan-Wilson's recent and important publication *Fray: Art and Textile Politics* (2018) takes the concept of frayed and fraying cloth as a means by which to consider the politics of textile culture. She turns to a wide range of cultural theorists and a selection of global artefacts. The breadth of material covered by Bryan-Wilson draws attention to neglected histories and ways in which these address textile practice and theory. Textiles often exist within a place between private and public, where the edges of both fray, or as Bryan-Wilson notes 'a queer place that transgresses the border between the sites of erotic activity and art-making' (2018: 74). In deconstructing fabric as a means of commenting on textile practices for marginalized groups, Bryan-Wilson focuses upon the potency of the fray.

As the selvedge gives way to a frayed edge, the structure of the cloth becomes revealed by parts. Echoing this, effective translation can only be effected through such a broken, jagged edge of uncertainty, where meaning can be reconstructed. In order to discuss these themes in terms of textile practice and its specific ability to articulate such syntactical frayage, the work of Isabel Wyrwa, Kristi Swee Kuder and Miram Medrez will be taken as key points of departure. In Izabela Wyrwa's delicate fabric and thread constructions, the jagged edges give way to entry at those points of frayage; they hover in space, balancing between the tangible and the elusive. Where Wyrwa constructs ephemeral forms that threaten to fray and fragment, American artist, Kristi Swee Kuder deconstructs woven stainless-steel mesh, drawing upon its frayed forms, its 'memory' of being woven, as a metaphor for the ways in which language defines and yet is often inadequate in the face of human experience. By way of forming a triangulation of these themes, the Mexican artist, Miriam Medrez will be a third focal point here. Medrez's work takes up the themes of frayed and fraying cloth as a means by which to consider ways in which the female body needs to constantly articulate itself at the frayed edges of language and culture. Using fraying textiles and inverted forms Medrez challenges the visibility of feminine praxis through a tactic of aesthetics and caretaking. Through these three artists, I want to highlight the role of textile practice and theory in making 'symbolically and materially . . . the tangible things that surround bodies and that organise, structure and lend meaning to the contours of everyday life' (Bryan-Wilson 2018: 41).

When cloth frays, its construction becomes revealed; warp and weft slip away from one another. In the same way that Vervoordt's exhibition concept privileges the hiatus, so the frayed cloth offers a tangible model for ways in which language and meaning can also cross and slip between users. The fraying edges of both cloth and language suggest a porous space of exchange and encounter.

Gayatri Spivak's explorations of the creative potential at the edges of language (1993: 200–25) offer a starting point for thinking through fraying. Elaine Showalter's essay 'Piecing and Writing' (1988) will be brought into play, particularly considering ways in which the practice of quilt-making can be thought of in terms of a model for thinking about modes of and for writing. This chapter proposes to focus upon forms of frayed and fraying textile practice and texts. There will be loose ends and thinning sections. Such frayage provokes thoughts concerned with mending and repair: decision-making about whether to darn and mend, to re-hem or to leave the frayed edges free. In other words, I am proposing the creation of a space for meaning to be made and of gaps where slippages of meaning encourage discussion and debate. I want to suggest that frayed and fraying offers a model for thinking and thinking-through-textile practice in which understanding emerges through negotiation and conversation: the frayed and fraying sections are identified, explored, negotiated and debated. Sometimes they are mended or darned, but sometimes left frayed as a conscious tactic of aesthetics or memory.

Frayed and fraying: A politics of translation

The literary theorist and philosopher Gayatri Spivak considers the politics of translation, positioning it within a context in which language is one of the many elements that allow us to make sense of the world or, for Spivak, 'the process of meaning-construction' (1993: 200) For her, language extends beyond words and phrases to encompass gestures and pauses, serendipities and encounters, and it is these elements of language, when brought together, that produce identity 'as self-meaning'. Thus, she proposes an extension to meaning-making in which language is simultaneously an expression of identity at the same time as it is a partner in the creation of that identity. In this then, she considers language to be 'a vital clue to where the self loses its boundaries' (202).

In thinking about the frayed edges of language, Spivak warns that it is at once both a dangerous and productive space, foregrounding its spaces, voids and multiple potentialities. In this she addresses the incompleteness of language. Thus, among the frayed edges of language meaning, meaning-making and identity become an extended form of dialogue, one which champions the coexistence and difference between *langue* (language) and *parole* (speaking).

Returning to the term frayage or 'facilitations', which is the English translation of the Freudian term *Bahnung*, Spivak refers to the neurological excitation caused by a new brain pattern meeting resistance. In habituation or assimilation, the passage of the neural transmission becomes 'learned' and is known as a facilitation or frayage which further excitations will continue to favour. For Spivak this marks a form of 'surrender' to the known. In this context translation involves a loss or breaking down of boundaries, a necessity in enabling dissemination. Occurring at the edges of language or between languages, frayage causes 'meaning [to] hop into the spacy emptiness between' (Spivak 1993: 398).

Spivak's translator, working on the edge of such spacy emptiness, where meaning can be both threatened and produced, juggles the 'disruptive rhetoricity that breaks the surface' (202). Here the selvedge gives way to a frayed edge and the structure of both languages becomes revealed by parts as the warp and weft of language slip away from each other. Effective translation, or communication between languages, takes place once the 'jagged relationship between rhetoric and logic, condition and effect of knowing' are reconfigured in the other language. The breaking down, or frayage, of the edges of language is a necessary part of the process: the translator must lay bare the structures of both languages, cut away the selvedges of language, which maintain exactitude of meaning, to produce frayages or excitations.

To think of frayed or fraying language in this way is to turn away from the idea that translation and understanding between languages and meaning-making bodies is an exact practice. Rather it is a spacy or holey place where the structure or the weave must be disturbed – a spacy emptiness that operates outside of phallocentric language systems.

Following a cloth-based mode of thinking Elaine Showalter, in her essay 'Piecing and Writing' (1985) compares the structural similarities of the quilt and short story, suggesting that American women's writing (and our reading of it) finds structural templates in quilt-making:

> I would like to suggest that a knowledge of piecing, the technique of assembling fragments into an intricate and ingenious design, can provide the contexts in which we can interpret and understand the forms, meanings and narrative traditions of American women's writing.
>
> (SHOWALTER IN MILLER 1986: 227)

While problematic in its potential for essentializing women's writing, Showalter's writing-quilt proposes a set of alternatives to the singular, author-led narrative. This mirroring of quilting with writing can be seen in terms of the kinds of units of time available to women. These are often characterized as creative work or acts of creation that are capable of surviving multiple interruptions for both the writer and the reader. However, *l'écriture féminine* and Cixous argue that woman has always been in a position of otherness and alterity within Western phallocentric culture (1976: 887) thus suggesting a decentred position from which to write. This could be framed as a multicentred patchwork of positions, a potentially uncontrolled or holey space of creation. Cixous suggests a writing from the body, but to think of that body as operating across the multicentred patchwork of fragments, complete with their frayed edges, or spacy emptiness, is to think about a space where Spivak's meaning can hop in.

Bryan-Wilson also turns to the quilt, specifically the AIDS Quilt, to consider the ways in which textile's flexibility offers a space for queering of practice or as she puts it, 'a polyvocal site of conflict' (2018: 250). The AIDS Quilt is often viewed as an embarrassment academically for its kitsch, déclassé, rough and imperfect appearance and finish. The Quilt, in its inelegant, amateur and inconvenient way, is the frayed edge of expression. It is, as Bryan-Wilson suggests, 'inherently neither "radical" nor "conservative", but poised, in tension, somewhere between' (249). The Quilt became a polarizing object in the 1980s and 1990s as a result of textile's pliancy or ability to fray and yield up meaning through its contradictions and erasures. Like a conventional bed quilt, it is patched and pieced, layered and pierced through with stitches. It disrupts and questions.

It is the unruliness that emerges from the AIDS Quilt that lends this set of textile-based forms their potency. The Quilt became a major platform for talking about the AIDS crisis at national and international levels, but it was not always received as a success, and was referred to as a 'miserable failure' (De Luca et al in Morris 2011: 627). It remains a provocative piece, but one that came into being through a range of activities aimed at naming and honouring those dying from AIDS and at the same time to counter a national rhetoric that this was a gay disease and thus at the margins of national interest. Nancy Gildart talks about such an impetus in terms of 'textile actions' (Livingstone and Ploof 2007: 241), actions that demarcate and establish social space and expression. In this sense, such actions and their products operate in the place of language and translation through the solidarity of contributed labour.

Donna Haraway, in her essay 'Situated Knowledges' (1988), suggests that embodied writing offers a form of privilege, a privilege of partial perspective, something she refers to as 'positioned rationality' (590). In this sense, then it is not about viewing from above as with maps and plans and the associated notions of escape or transcendence of limits and borders that this might offer, but rather about 'the joining of partial views and halting voices into a collective subject position' (590). Here again is the notion of solidarity and of joining pieces, patching and piecing of text, voices and language. The pieces don't point back to a single point of origin, nor are they constructed around a singular narrative. The patchwork quilt as the model allows for the pieces to operate together as traces or an index that relate to each other by contiguity. Such a way of thinking offers frayage, or the breaking down of the selvedge (the self-edge) as a progressive tactic. It disrupts the regressive search for an origin, acting as a tactic which points not to the outcome of the activity, but upon revealing the form of the structure.

Frayed and fraying cloth: Broken and contingent

There exists in the material culture of everyday life a particular role for cloth as an expression and embodiment of identity. Cloth as material, both physically and culturally, possesses specific qualities such as softness, fluidity and an ability to become imbued with memories that can be utilized at transitional or fraying stages of development, offering direct sensory experiencing alongside metaphoric expression of that transitional process. While these statements could be made about a number of other artefacts, cloth's material and metaphorical particularity together with its associations with the body open it out as a potent interpretative and expressive tool.

Frayed and fraying cloth, broken and tentative, offers a powerful metaphor for both the transitional object and process. Psychoanalyst Melanie Klein, building on Freud's theories of childhood development, articulates a prehistory which outlines a sequence of events leading to the infant's integration of the real world with its own chaotic desiring world. The Kleinian model of 'object relations' sets the infant's world as one threatened by anxieties that stem from the infant's death instinct, being felt in the infant's own bodily needs. Such overwhelming anxieties are combatted by the infant through primitive defences: projection, denial, splitting and control over external objects. This latter involves setting 'bad' objects outside and into the external world, while preserving 'good' objects internally. These early objects are anything that is not the self: not-me objects and even part-objects such as one of the mother's breasts (Klein 1957: 68).

Paediatrician and psychoanalyst Donald Winnicott suggested in his paper 'Transitional Objects and Transitional Phenomena: A Study of the First Not-Me Possession' (1953) that the 'transitional object' acts as mediating tissue between the infant and the external world at the point of recognition of separateness from the m(other) (Winnicott 1953: 89). This object, exemplified by a baby's blanket or sheet, is a defence against anxiety and becomes absolutely necessary at moments of loneliness or when a depressed moment looms (Winnicott 1953: 91). It comes into play when there arises a sense that the continuum between infant and mother is becoming fragmented and frayed.

In replacing the part-object such as the breast with this 'not-me' possession there occurs an element of frayage at the borderline between subject and object, both on a symbolic level and as a social relation. It is through this object that such relations are first experienced as such by the infant. In this sense, it is its material reality as not– m(other) that is as important as its symbolic presence as the m(other) (Winnicott 1953: 92) and thus gives room for the process of becoming able to accept that separation. The transitional object, then, is a form of frayed and fraying cloth, whose selvedge has become broken to reveal the structural elements and process. As frayed cloth, the transitional object, according to Winnicott, is the visible aspect of the infant's inner 'journey from the purely subjective to objectivity' (1953: 92) and cloth objects are, as a result of both proximity and intimate relationship with the body, readily taken up for this role.

Winnicott's illustration of his theory with textile objects could be considered incidental, but I want to suggest here that focusing upon textile, together with its physical, proximal and cultural materiality, opens up a space for thinking through its ability to affect changes in object/subject relations that corresponds to formative and transitory aspects of the formation of identity. In formal psychoanalytic terms, the notion of textile as a medium of and for creativity and as a transitional or frayed object within that capacity, offers the potential for the artist and viewer to draw on the artwork to navigate the complexities of the world together and separately. This is not to posit the work of the creative drive as therapeutic activity, but rather as an ongoing means by which to negotiate the balancing of desires and drives.

Claire Pajaczkowska, in her essay 'Making Known: the textiles toolbox – psychoanalysis of nine types of textile thinking' (in Jefferies et al. 2016: 72–92), takes up these ideas to consider ways in which making with textiles is simultaneously making the self and making society. She suggests that this implicates the role of empathy, which both Winnicott's and Klein's objects require for their potency. Pajaczkowska also points to the role of violence and destruction in the ontology of the artefact (82) which overcomes romanticized approaches, but offers a means for thinking through the role of fraying within textile practice. In this sense, she sets making as praxis, but it is a praxis with something of the undisciplined through its relational foundations. Without the selvedge, cloth frays and deconstructs itself, returning to its material elements.

I want to suggest that textile as art object is the transitional object for the artist which offers an extension to Winnicott's theory in that the artist actively creates the object and thus has greater control over both signifier and signified at the point of production. Within the relationship between artist and art object textile, in its materiality and with its ability to operate as agency of formation as well as expression, is particularly potent. If, as Roland Barthes suggests, text is made generatively 'in a perpetual interweaving' (1973: 64) or transitional space of mania and oceanic bliss, then text and textile here fray at their edges, becoming transitional objects or phenomena as the artist and textile enter into a process of cathexis[1] or frayage which transforms both in active participation. Further, in the haptic engagement with the object, there is necessarily involved a notion of possession of that object which is vital for it to be transitional in Winnicott's terms and thus for it to fray, and in so doing bridge the gap between internal and external, subject and object. In this sense, it belongs to both the internal and external realms being neither under magical control (internal) nor beyond control as the m(other) (external) (Winnicott 1953: 94). The transformation that takes place and thus makes a transitional object out of some ubiquitous and ephemeral object of the infant's life (as far as the parent is concerned) is a participatory act of creation on the part of the infant. This ephemerality is an important factor in the transitional object and the items exemplified by Winnicott will all fray when subjected to the kinds of behaviour he describes (1953: 92), which assists their demise or apparent re-introjection at the appropriate stage.

To think of the transitional object in terms of frayed and fraying cloth moves beyond textile as a paradigmatic form and allows for a fuller potency to be revealed. In order to consider this further I want to focus upon the work of Izabela Wyrwa, whose delicate fabric and thread constructions fray and fragment and yet continue to define a voluminous presence. Their jagged edges hover in space, balancing between the tangible and the elusive. *Co´s w Powietrzu/Something in the Air* (2010) (Plate 17) offers an example of the ways in which frayed and fraying cloth as practice operates within the not-me space of the transitional object.

Co´s w Powietrzu is, for Wyrwa, 'an example of subject affective states in real space' (artist's statement, June 2016). The transparent fabrics and threads take on forms that are fleeting, more gestural than realized forms. The fragments are held together delicately, as if placed temporarily against one another. The form and tension is created through its installation, fixed at points so that in different spaces the texture and weight shift and change. The structural form at the centre of the work becomes clearly defined, making a contrast with the edges. The form suggests spatial qualities, moving from specific reference points towards frayed and fragmented, indeterminate boundaries.

The play of light brings drama of shadow and movement, emphasizing the structural forms and re-defining the space the work occupies. Wyrwas's work and its materials make visible the delicate touch of air, its affect, but without giving the viewer a sense of completion – it is an ongoing affect.

Pajaczkowska's proposal for a rehabilitation of textile making addresses the possibility of the transitional object becoming paraphrased as a 'comfort object' in that it supports the transitory phases of development. However, its potency, and that of cloth, lies in the gestures of that attachment and its wearing out or frayage as part of that intermediary space. It operates in the play between conceived and actual experiencing of the world. In this way Wyrwa's hovering installations, with their tentative edges become that intermediate space, marking the movement from unification out into separatedness. In this sense, such works as *Co´s w Powietrzu* become more than its spatial qualities, more than its lightness and ephemerality. The work is about the gestures that brought them into being as a form of exercise of oneself. They are almost objects, but not quite; it is as if they have taken up the very form of what we are called to learn to be separate from. The work is almost spectral in this sense.

The act of bringing an artwork into being could be considered to be a form of transitional gesture, in the sense that there comes a point in the process of creativity at which a form of conversation or communication occurs between the artwork and artist: a point of frayage or separation emerges. In her experiments with free drawing, Wyrwa's drawings take on a form of dialogic relationship between thought and the bit of the external world represented by the marks in space. This form of dialogue requires the movement or gesture that marks a differentiation between self and artwork and thus the artwork at this stage could be considered in terms of a frayed practice in which another emerges from the self with its own desires and demands, even though it emerges from within the artist.

In Wyrwa's work stains and gestures carry affective value which mimics the role of the transitional object. For Wyrwa textile as art object suggests a screen or site for mingling or weaving together perception and expression. In this she could be seen, through her use of textile as transitional, frayed, creative object and process, to be recreating a state of existence that is now lost to her. Thus, the creative activity demonstrated through *Co´s w Powietrzu* occupies a psychodynamic role that extends beyond the figurative and tangible to enable passage into the frayed space in which the work seems to be doing itself.

In *Co´s w Powietrzu*, Wyrwa brings together abstraction and materiality, formulating the problematic posed by Marxist–feminist culture dividing and uniting productive labour and reproductive labour through the same textile objects in a mirroring and mimicking of the developing ego. It is in this sense that *Co´s w Powietrzu* can be read as a transitional object, not only for the artist but also for the viewer. In these textile objects the boundary of the self frays and unleashes itself from a I/Not-I binary. This work situates Wyrwa and viewer together, as subject and thus the work frays the edges of subject and object, artist and viewer in a reversal of

the infant's transitional object as established by Winnicott in the activity of creativity that brought it into being. Here, in the frayed forms is the remnant of the transitional object, worn away by repeated touching that reveals its structural elements.

Textile as transitional art object has the potential to operate as that first not-me possession where artist/viewer assumes rights over the object and meaning derived from it and as such is subject to change only by that artist/ viewer. Through its frayed and fraying edges, it bridges the gap between inside and outside, subject and object, never fully belonging to either realm of existence; the loosened threads become a threshold between biological and social self, a space of simultaneous connection and division. Within the warp and weft of Wyrwa's installation meaning has been imbued that gradually fades for the individual, not forgotten nor repressed, but diffused. Such frayage enables both artist and viewer to operate within the Real world where subject and object are separated, but its mediating tissue offers a window onto the subjectivity of the other and so to locate and navigate one's own desiring capacities. As the artist creates meaning out of the material of her own practice, the viewer is brought into transitional relationship with that subjectivity and thus is enabled, through the cultural and physical materiality of textile, to produce a generative space of signification for themselves through the process of frayage.

The body that performs and produces the *écriture féminine* that Haraway refers to is that of woman, a body that commonly operates as a form of boundary marker to cultural identity. Women's bodies are those that become veiled and the source of the male gaze, marking the boundary for communal purity and thus objects of social surveillance and control. Hamid Naficy characterizes this as a space from which both belonging and estrangement can operate, in which 'the critical juxtaposition of parallel spaces, times, voices, narratives and foci' promotes destabilization, deterritorialization or frayage at the edges (1999: 43–5).

Such frayage, however, offers a vision of both connection (or perhaps reconnection) and severance, a doubly attenuated locus, or perhaps series of loci, where Spivak's 'spacy emptiness' can be found momentarily. Haraway's terms suggest a reading of such a space as one of the partial, where connections, unexpected openings and situated knowledges are formed. It is thus a space foregrounded on contiguity, plurality and the revealing of structure by parts. So, to talk in terms of boundaries when speaking of positioned rationality is a risky project as that which they contain is by its very nature generative and productive and thus it spills out and over its own boundaries, fraying the edges, fraying and rupturing its centres as it burgeons forth.

Frayage offers a way of thinking beyond syntax and represents a fraught cross-cultural space within which transmission, translation and reception become problematized. The structures of meaning and meaning-making become partially and temporarily revealed to each other, the translator inculcated into the structural dialectic.

To the edge: Pointing away from the centre

In many ways, the frayed space of language can be thought of as a space of and for the visual artist to bring into being the work of art. It is a space that is extra-linguistic, it expands expression beyond words and into the self. To focus further upon that extra-linguistic space and its potential for expanding beyond itself, I want here to consider the work of American artist, Kristi Swee Kuder. Where Wyrwa constructs ephemeral forms that threaten to fray and fragment in their contingency, Kuder deconstructs woven steel mesh, drawing upon its frayed forms, its 'memory' of being woven, as a means by which to think about how language defines and at the same time is inadequate in the face of human experiencing.

This could be considered to be a nomadic sculptural form in which architectural and textile gestures come together at the point of the work's deconstruction, but also out in front of this in terms of their ability to materialize the dissonance between structure and order, destruction and disorder. In this way it becomes a meditation on building and rebuilding, suggesting forms that never completely coalesce into over-representation, becoming simultaneously a condition that exists between pre- and post-construction.

Here, then, Kuder operates in a fissure between material realization and abstraction, where the elements and forms are ambivalent, they playfully reassert their textile roots, while pointing towards the architectural and industrial. In some of her works the steel mesh is still intact, the mark of the loom's work still evident. In others warp is indistinguishable from weft. If a warp could be thought to be half of a weave or a weave half-removed, then the unravelled thread is suggestive of its 'mirroring' or absent weft, rendering the making of cloth visible and re-siting the notion of the activity of weaving within a gallery space. Kuder does not, however, present the viewer with the stages of the process of weaving, nor indeed is that her intention. Instead she offers the attentive viewer a compendium of fractured, partial and incomplete vignettes: is this a cloth in the throes of construction or has it been abandoned and decomposing, are the edges fraying?

In *Cold Fusion* (2014) (Plate 18), Kuder presents the viewer with a layered, transparent mesh box, the mesh frayed at the centre of each face so that the viewer can see through the entangled threads. In this she reanimates warp and weft. The disjunctive moments and moiré of layered mesh and the repeated forms together draw attention to the process of the mesh's construction, but also to the processes and preoccupations of such textile practice.

Cold Fusion playfully reanimates the ubiquitous and perceived quotidian practices and processes of making and mending. Kuder raises attention to what some might refer to as 'the crisis of production and skill-based textile labor' (Picard 2011: 8) and here, by using the frayed edges as frame, such preoccupations become the locus for thinking about making through a process of unmaking. Thus, in this work notions of making and unmaking considered as a binary are challenged: both co-reside here at the site of the material elements of textile practice. This could be considered in terms of indirection, not as a form of stasis, but rather Kuder's work and practice stands at the intersection between making and unmaking, as a form of performed potentiality. Process and structure become revealed within these works: in the minutest movements and gestures, in the warp and weft entangled on the precipice between reorder and chaos. The work does not offer resolution, but draws on the intimacy of textile, its materials and materiality as a strategy to reconfigure the interplay between process and art object, in a playing out of Pajaczkowska's call for a rearticulation of textile practice–theory discourse and protocols. In returning to textile as a transformative process, Kuder's work articulates its own praxis of textile.

Cold Fusion, in its deconstruction frays at its edges, and sets up spaces between process and production that suggest an immanent space of potentialities. Such a frayed edge reminds the viewer of the materiality and physicality of making, referring that viewer back to the artist-as-creator in an endless repetition of making/unmaking – in an echo of Barthes' *hyphology*.

As the cloth frays to reveal its structure, so too does Kuder's work reveal the relationship between production and artwork as one of repeated origins; in many ways it is a kind of undoing of movement forward, which is not regressive. Like the frayed cloth, the undoing does not reverse the process of weaving, so much as it sets warp and weft in a new, cohabiting relationship: attached where the cloth is unfrayed, but no longer bound together by a selvedge (or seam). Kuder's work highlights this altered relational infrastructure in which past, present and future constantly reframe themselves.

Thinking in terms of such a structure of making and thinking offers a structural form which Paul Carter suggests

> grows more superficial, more irrational, more mimetic. Its winding tendrils . . . show themselves capable of incorporating the most heterogenous forms and beliefs. Promiscuous cross-fertilisation and miscegenation replace tradition and influence as a means of generating new forms.
>
> (CARTER 2004: 2)

One of the characteristics of thinking about Kuder's work in such a way is that it enables the tangles of threads and the moiré effect in *Cold Fusion* to exist as contingent and temporary forms and structures. As the work presents both its making and unmaking, order and disorder, it circles back in a densely layered resonance between new and old technologies of making, handmade and industrial production. Further it echoes, rematerializes and affirms Kuder's preoccupations with materiality and the labour of production.

Thus, Kuder's work more broadly could be considered not as a series of works but as an ongoing site of concentrated physical activity. Perpetually provisional, her improvisations establish a useful and meaningful model for textile practice–theory interplay. They persistently point away from their centre, away from resolution, towards their frayed and fraying edges and uncertainty in the gestures of this fervent activity.

Worn through

Cloth does not only fray at the edges: it frays also where it becomes worn or overly rubbed, creating a thinness, that threatens the whole in quite a different way to the frayed or fraying edge. This thinness mirrors language and places where metaphor breaks down, where translation has to work across cultural gaps, spaces where the reader needs to replace the broken or thinned threads with those from their own cultural understanding. This again provides a space of danger and production, a space between languages and cultures, a space that is constantly at risk of separating or pulling away from the other.

Such a space can be thought about in terms of its frayed and worn form, where its function becomes compromised as a result of the weakened structure. Taken as such, the work or thinning cloth enters into a new relationship with the whole, unfrayed cloth. According to Derrida, 'writing offers only the repetition of knowledge, not its production through an act of remembering' (Derrida in Gebauer and Wulf 1992: 297). Thus, writing can only enter into relationship with knowing, it cannot produce it. The frayed and fraying cloth offers a reverse of this, returning writing to the body that produced it, the cloth back to the generative interplay between warp and weft.

This reversal is enabled as a result of the doubling or mirroring that occurs within the frayed/unfrayed relationship. Repetition points back to the original, while simultaneously locating its difference to that original, giving the new relationship past and future reference points in so doing.

To think of the relationship between textile practice and theory, then, could be said to be, like the cloth wearing thin at the centre, a key moment in the process of deconstruction that reveals its construction and the process. As warp and weft thin and separate, so they become new points of departure. These lines of flight, as Deleuze and Guattari would call them, or freed threads, enable a new mode of knowledge production, one based upon difference, distinctions, delimitations and the possibility of new combinations. In contrast to imitation or reproduction, what this offers is indeterminacy, oscillation and displacement.

What is at play when thinking in terms of wearing thin is the potentiality of the frayed relationship, as a combination of elements, free to enter into a new relationship. As warp and weft are held together within the woven cloth, when worn and thinned, they separate and the interplay between them becomes revealed: in the absence of the structuring scaffold of the cloth, its material presence becomes revealed.

Through the relationship of worn with whole cloth, similarities and difference engage in mimetic play with each other in an elliptical landscape: wholeness can never be restored to the cloth frayed at the centre, it can never be assimilated back into the whole cloth landscape. This could be thought of as a form of paradoxical logic which is

> characterised by breaks, concentrations and displacements; they run up against empty spaces in which there is neither subject nor properties; they flow into paradoxical constellations in which contradictions combine with each other in mimetic play.
>
> (GEBAUER AND WULF 1992: 307)

This notion of mimetic interplay, repetition and frayed centres and the inherent danger of collapse places an accent upon ideas of dissidence from within a disciplinary or organizing system. The artwork of Mexican artist Miriam Medrez takes up the themes of frayed and fraying cloth as a means by which to consider the need for the female body to be repeatedly rearticulated at the frayed edges of language and culture.

Medrez's work is figurative and expressionistic, filed with female figures sometimes seemingly engaged in everyday activities and at others caught in moments of suspended concentration. In the series *Zurciendo (Mending)* (2010) (Plates 19 and 20), this bodily presence is a constant. The fabric figures are soft and frayed at the knees, over the scalp and down the back. The figures appear and re-appear throughout the series, never quite the same, but never idiosyncratic enough to maintain a sense of differentiation that comes with figurative work. In this they mimic warp and weft, under and over repeated.

In Medrez's hands these nearly repeated series of figures take on a temporal, somewhat filmic sense. The temporal order here is concerned with both succession and simultaneity, while resisting hierarchy and narrative structures. As she selects fabric pieces, joining them firstly together in sections and then into blocks to make the forms, so Medrez constructs her assemblages. Each individual figure is carefully composed, forming its own locus, which is linked to the others in the series.

Zurciendo (Mending) can be framed in terms of Deleuze & Guattari's 'assemblage', which they loosely describe as ad hoc groupings or collections of diverse elements, constituted from vibrant material of all sorts. Deleuze and Guattari continue to suggest that an assemblage is an event-space that has no head, no organizing principle, remaining an open-ended collective, forever threatening to disperse or disintegrate. The constituent parts or members of an assemblage are held together temporarily within its force field. Constantly in formation and reformation, these members adopt a strategy of multiple determinations that cannot be reduced to a single logic. The assemblage produces difference which suggests an assemblage could be thought of as a living, shifting system of being that functions despite the consistent and persistent internal energies that threaten to disrupt the unifying force field. Thinking of the woven cloth as an assemblage envisions a structure held together by the weft threads that wrap around the selvedge. Once threads are broken or worn through, warp and weft pull apart and the rectilinear structure established upon the loom breaks down, revealing the contingent nature of that structure, while also enabling the now-fraying cloth to shift and move in new ways. As Medrez's figures reveal and deny themselves through both difference and repetition, they also continuously repeat the contradictions of the female body: she is simultaneously public and anonymous, private and personal, rebellious and subversive. She frays the network that she has constructed, revealing what could be conceived of as the figure's hypocrisy within her compositions.

Dispensing with the portrait's figure in favour of anonymity, Medrez is able to focus upon the peripheral elements: carpets, curtains, plants and drapery, rebelliously subverting and transposing their roles in a mirroring of the portrait. In *Zurceindo (Mending)*, she works in monochrome, to produce a series of cloth portraits which dwell on the essence of their woven and uncoloured characteristics. These individually encapsulated compositions come together in assemblage. Part animation, part still-life, these portraits vibrate between figure and ground, fraying from their bodies' surfaces thus attempting to escape themselves. The abstract and representational fall together where the structure frays, seemingly part of a larger performative act, an act that reveals itself not in terms of production, but rather in terms of affect or a form of agency. This agency of the assemblage, because of its transient and temporary status, is a shifting, pulsating energy which changes over time as the frayed centre enables internal reorganization. When the threads become loosened from those with which they were intertwined at the site of the frayage, they can form new sets of relationships within the assemblage and be drawn together within a different set of allies. This creative potential and performative activity within threatens its integrity and subverts notions of fixed and permanent structures/institutions, but at the same time enables a flexibility and manoeuvrability. As the cloth frays and wears thin from the centre, it retains part of its previous form, while also becoming increasingly porous and tenuous.

In thinking of Medrez's work in terms of both assemblage and fraying at the centre, it is possible to make the ground the subject of the work, while also offering a commentary on that shift from figure to ground. The ground becomes a form of theatre in which the fabric takes centre stage and folds, undulates and collapses within its loosely bounded space. As a whole assemblage, the multiple movements or stagings, become animated, breaking out of the confines Medrez constructs and connecting and reconnecting with each other. The frayed and thinning edges and surfaces allow for movement left to right, right to left, up, down and around, with new movements being created at every turn. Thus, the frayed centre, worn through, offers passage to and fro between the rectilinear and the baroque, with its folds, foldings and re-foldings, always multiple, always in transit.

The play here between boundary and frayed surfaces causes the work to be somewhat claustrophobic, the result of pedantic meticulousness, perhaps. But I would argue that in her focus upon the structuring of the portrait, the insularity of the work frays itself, drawing the viewer into the internal relationships between elements. As the monochrome threads and fabrics, forms and prostheses, play between figure and ground within the work seep between each other and secrete movement from their performative inception. Repetition weaves between these pieces within the structural chain of the assemblage.

Fraying

When cloth frays, its construction becomes revealed, offering a metaphor for ways in which language and meaning can cross and slip between users in an expression of meaning-making. Thinking through frayed and fraying cloth, the relationship between textile practice and theory becomes a porous space for both to co-mingle and co-produce meaning and expression.

In this chapter, there has been a focus upon forms and processes of fraying and the potential effects and affects of those processes on the worn and broken cloth. There are loose ends and thinning sections that emerge in the creation of an assemblage within which the fraying centre requires and enables realignment of meaning beyond translation.

For Spivak, the frayed and fraying edges of language offer a space of both danger and production, where the gaps encourage extra-linguistic modes for understanding. Showalter capitalizes on these concepts in her piecing and writing model, taking patchwork pieces and making from them a quilt whose organizing principle is not that of the narrative, but rather a decentred, frayed and mingling coming together. Such a model is one which celebrates the fragmented, frayed and holey for the ability of such sites to allow meaning to be made within them. This is where Spivak's meaning hops in. Haraway suggests that such spacy emptiness offers the privilege of partial perspective. Fraying and frayage then could be said to point to a way beyond syntax, suggesting that the textile practice–theory space is fraught and needs to be negotiated and renegotiated repeatedly. At such sites the structural elements are both disturbed and revealed, offering a model based on decentred and fragmented writing that could be considered to be Haraway's progressive tactic for making meaning or Pajaczkowska's 'making known' (in Jefferies et al 2016: 92).

To think of the relationship between textile practice and theory through fraying and frayage is to think about the edges of each being fragmented and broken or to think of the cloth worn thin through use at its centre. This chapter has considered both of these in turn, focusing particularly on how these forms of frayage alter and shift the relationship between centre and edge. The frayed edge, as a mode of thinking, is not predicated upon the notion of resolution, but rather upon uncertainty and the associated fervent activity that surrounds this. The frayed edge, having revealed the structure of the cloth to be one of mutual dependency, threatens the integrity of the whole and as such establishes a site that is perpetually provisional and in danger. Warp and weft could continue to separate and the cloth would cease to be, the centre would momentarily become an edge before it too frayed and returned to being separated threads. Kuder's *Cold Fusion* takes on a playful assertion, this time between itself as textile and as industrial product. The playfulness of un-knowing becomes a repeated aspect of the work but, in their fraying, there is no return to stability and meaning established remains contingent.

The metaphor of thinning and fraying cloth brought about by wear and use at the centre opens up a different set of relationships between centre and edge in which stability is threatened from within. This mimics mimesis, offering the metaphor as a doubling and reproductive form of mimesis. Thus, when the centre starts to fray, there is an inherent and inevitable danger of collapse inwards, something Medrez explores in her figurative compositions. Like Deleuze and Guattari's assemblage, these artworks are held together through multiple determinations and are forever at risk of dispersal. The grid promises stability and certainty of meaning, but from within the lines of the grid emerges perpetual difference and dissonance. These small theatrical spaces set the fabric drapery in a new role as both foreground and background, enabling its characteristics to become animated and activated. Through this they come together to form a performative space that breaks down the grid as if it were a worn-out piece of cloth and the individual undulations and syncopations of the cloth in movement become revealed.

TRA, Vervoordt suggests, can be thought of as 'a gateway between worlds' (2011: 3) and thus a threshold must be breached in order to reveal a new landscape. This sets the threshold as the edge of becoming, a propositional space with connections running towards and away from the frayed edge and centre. As the cloth's structure becomes revealed, so too can ways into and beyond the whole cloth be seen and explored. The spaces and gaps between offer ways for thinking-through-practice and theory, writing and making, text and textile.

PLATES

Plate 1 Jane Lackey, *Enveloping Space: Walk, Trace, Think*, 2014. Site-specific installation, spector ripps project space, Center for Contemporary Art, Santa Fe, New Mexico, 1,000 sq. ft. Photo: Jane Lackey.

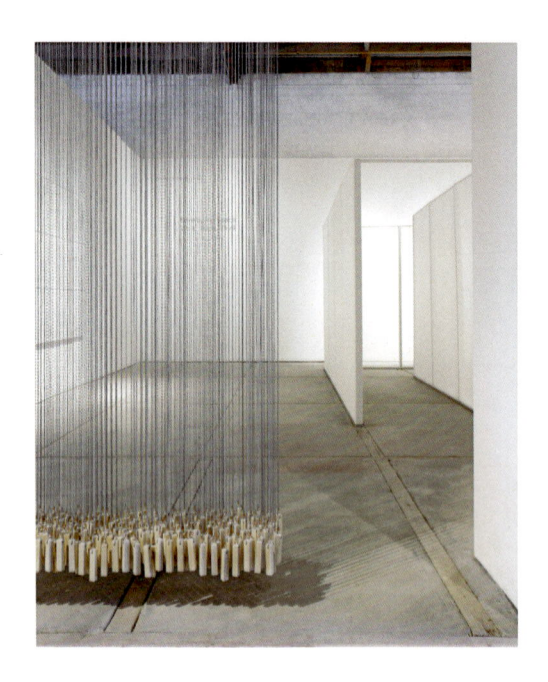

Plate 2 Jane Lackey, *Enveloping Space: Walk, Trace, Think*, 2014. Threshold: nylon cord, pine, copper crimps, rubber bands, MDF board. Photo: Jane Lackey.

Plate 3 Jane Lackey, *Enveloping Space: Walk, Trace, Think*, 2014. Swipe wall and enclosed writing space: wool felt, chalk powder, MDF, polyester voile fabric, poplar, paint. Photo: Jane Lackey.

Plate 4 Eva Hesse, *Right After*, 1969. Drawing, Private Collection. Photo: Private Collection, New York © The Estate of Eva Hesse.

Plate 5 Eva Hesse, *Right After*, 1969. Fibreglass, approximately: 5 × 18 × 4 ft (152.39 × 548.61 × 121.91 cm). Milwaukee Art Museum, Gift of Friends of Art. M1970.27 © The Estate of Eva Hesse. Courtesy Hauser & Wirth.

Plate 6 Eva Hesse, *Right After*, 1969. Fibreglass, approximately: 5 × 18 × 4 ft (152.39 × 548.61 × 121.91 cm). Milwaukee Art Museum, Gift of Friends of Art. M1970.27 © The Estate of Eva Hesse. Courtesy Hauser & Wirth.

Plate 7 Tricia Middleton, *Troubles with Boundaries*, 2017 (detail) mixed media, found objects, cloth. Installation dimensions variable. Photo: Paul Nicoué.

Plate 8 Tricia Middleton, *Troubles with Boundaries*, 2017 (detail) mixed media, found objects, cloth. Installation dimensions variable. Photo: Paul Nicoué.

Plate 9 Ann Hamilton, *human carriage*, 2009. Installation, The Third Mind: American Artists Contemplate Asia: 1860–1989. Solomon R. Guggenheim Museum, New York. 30 January 2009–19 April 2009. Photo: Thibault Jeanson.

Plate 10 Ann Hamilton, *human carriage*, 2009. Installation, The Third Mind: American Artists Contemplate Asia: 1860–1989. Solomon R. Guggenheim Museum, New York. 30 January 2009–19 April 2009. Photo: Thibault Jeanson.

Plate 11 Kirstie MacLeod, *The Red Dress* (2009–), installation, dimensions variable. Photo: Dave Watts.

Plate 12 Kirstie MacLeod, *The Red Dress* (2009–), installation, dimensions variable. Photo: Nicole Esselen.

Plate 13 Rosalind Wyatt, *A boy who loved to run* (2013). Stitched running vest. Photo: MLR Photo.

Plate 14 Rosalind Wyatt, *A boy who loved to run* (2013). Stitched running vest. Photo: MLR Photo.

Plate 15 Chiharu Shiota, *After the Dream* (2009) © DACS 2015.

Plate 16 Chiharu Shiota, *After the Dream* (2009) © DACS 2015.

Plate 17 Izabel Wyrwa. *Something in the Air* (2010), installation. Wire, aluminium net, synthetic materials. Property of the artist. Photo: Izabel Wyrwa.

Plate 18 Kristi Kuder, *Cold Fusion* (2016), stainless-steel mesh, acrylic rods, beads 20"w × 23"h × 20"d.

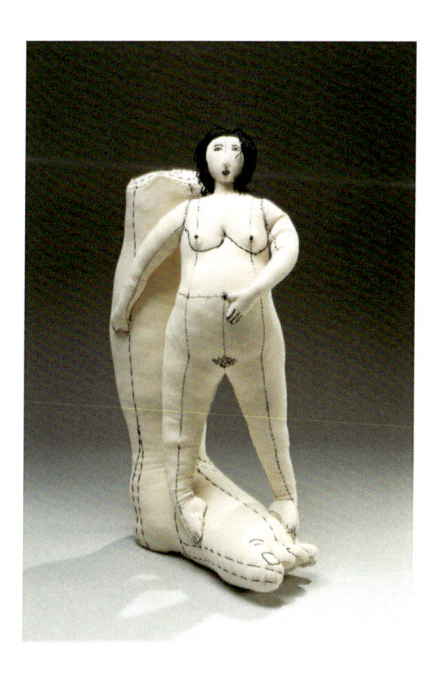

Plate 19 Miriam Medrez, *Zurciendo (Mending)* (2010), installation. Cloth, black thread, scissors, needle, ruler, paper and pencil. Photo: Roberto Ortis © Miriam Medrez.

Plate 20 Miriam Medrez, *Zurciendo (Mending)* (2010), installation. Cloth, black thread, scissors, needle, ruler, paper and pencil. Photo: Roberto Ortis © Miriam Medrez.

Plate 21 Kari Steihaug, *After the Market* (2009), installation. Size variable, unravelled knitted wool clothes/knitted image after the painting *The Gleaners* (1857), Jean-Francois Millet. Photo: M Tomaszewicz. Courtesy: The National Museum of Art, Architecture and Design, Norway.

Plate 22 Kari Steihaug, *Legacies* (2006), installation. Size variable, unravelled knitted wool clothes, spools of yarn, knitted sweater. Contemporary Art Center, Cincinnati, Ohio, 2016. Photo: Courtesy of the Contemporary Arts Center © Tony Walsh Photography.

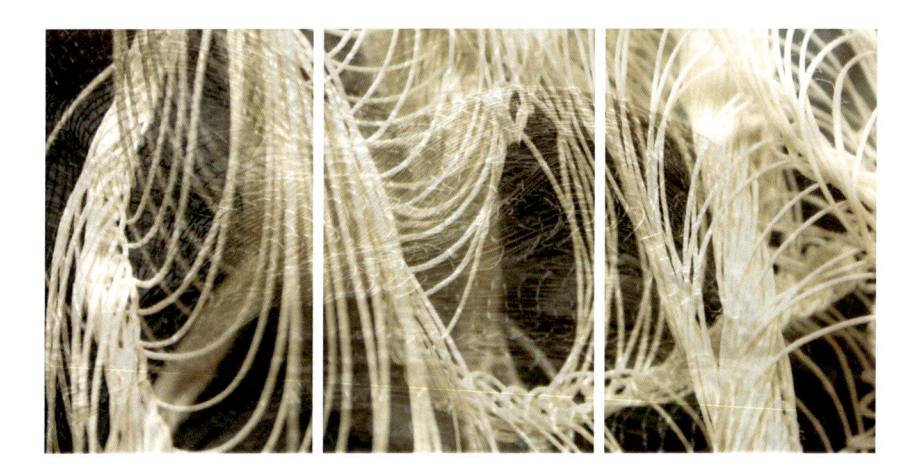

Plate 23 Catherine Dormor, *Warp & Waft* (2016), digital print on silk satin and silk organza. Each 120 x 240 x 30 cm. Photo: Catherine Dormor.

Plate 24 Catherine Dormor, *Warp & Waft 2* (2016), digital print on silk satin and silk organza. Each 120 × 240 × 30 cm. Photo: Catherine Dormor.

Plate 25 Stephanie Metz. Installation view, *Flesh & Bone* wool sculptures, ArtArk Gallery, San Jose, California. Photo by Stephanie Metz.

Plate 26 Stephanie Metz. *Amorphozoa #1.2*, wool, 15 cm × 16.5 cm × 27 cm, 2014. Photo by Stephanie Metz.

6
TEXTILE AS CARESSING SUBJECT/OBJECT

The caress consists in seizing upon nothing in soliciting what slips away as though it were not yet. It searches, it forages. It is not an intentionality of disclosure, but of search: a movement into the invisible.
(LÉVINAS 1969: 257–8)

The female body in Western culture is often seen, and treated, as a repository, holder or pocket. This draws on Freud's perspective that the post-oedipal female body is first and foremost a home for the phallus and subsequently a baby; without these it is incomplete and a violation (Freud 1933: 133). In this sense, the female body as a site for and of touch, or the caress: a gentle touch or gesture of fondness, tenderness or love (*OED*) is a site to be 'completed' by the male body, most specifically by that phallus. This locates heterosexual intercourse as the locus classicus of relationships between the sexes and thus the role of the caress operates as the precursor to (male) sexual gratification – a means to an end within a polarized or power-based male–female relationship. So, whereas the caress is defined as 'a loving touch' it operates in practice as a pre-intercourse mode of arousal.

Jean-Paul Sartre, in *Being and Nothingness* (1943), does nothing to dispel such phallocentric ideas and ideologies in his discussion of the object of desire as 'maybe now a slice of bread, now an automobile, now a woman' (Sartre 1943: 596).

Positing of the female body as an object of desire among a range, to be had or possessed by the male body, affords the female body no space to be a desiring body, and so a new way of thinking is needed in order to be able to fully open up what it might mean to be that female body in the world. To think about the female body as a desiring body opens up a discourse in which it becomes a form of conceptual framework for thinking about and making meaning of and in the world.

It is thus from the female body that this chapter explores the notion of the caress, and its associations with textile and cloth, as a means for reflecting upon textile as both a practice and a set of theories. This is a means by which to think in extended ways about desire, and the caress in particular as an expression of that desire, that are not foregrounded by the idea of *objects* of desire as routes to male gratification. Thus, this is not Freud's female body as the home for the phallus, but rather this is the female body whose difference from the male body becomes a source of communication between bodies and which stresses the prefix *com–* (together, with), and exchange, and thus foregrounds the porosity bound up in difference rather than othering. This posits the caress as an end in itself within that libidinal exchange between two.

The notion of the caress as a form of porous communication between two is addressed within this chapter under four key themes: *proximity*, which highlights the need for an openness prior to contact as part of a caress-as-gesture; *opening out – becoming . . .*, which focuses upon textile artist Kari Steihaug to develop the physical and structural activity of the caress at the site of the skin and way(s) in which differing philosophical and phenomenological models of touch interrelate with the notion of the caress; the third theme, *measuring distance,* considers the artwork of Stephanie Metz to draw together metaphorical and physical notions of proximity; in the final section, *first actions of hands*, my own textile works will be foregrounded to highlight the caress as primal gesture that has multiple origins and which suggests an expanded mode of being two.

To think of the caress as a model for textile practice is to think of the cloth's woven structure as a form of reciprocal awakening of warp and weft, a term drawn from Luce Irigaray's search for a language of the caress. This mirrors cloth's role as a primal site of the caress through clothing most often. It acts as stimulus to the body and produces a generative encounter between the cloth and body.

Affective touching

The caress is a gesture-word which goes beyond the horizon or the distance of intimacy within the self. This is true for the one who is caressed and touched, for the one who is approached within the sphere of his or her incarnation, but it is also true for the one who caresses, for the one who touches and accepts distancing the self from the self through this gesture.

(IRIGARAY 2000: 26)

Irigaray's notion of the caress as a relational gesture-word offers a way of thinking about tactility and tactile (inter)relationships as offering intimate spaces of difference. This focuses upon intimate affectivity. In his enticingly titled essay, 'Caresses, Excesses, Intimacies and Estrangements' (2004), where one might anticipate find the caress as gesture, Mark Paterson turns to the metaphor or narrative of a hotel room encounter to ponder whether the caress is anything but prehension, a grasping or groping for meaning (173). He turns to Lévinas and Irigaray who when taken together locate within the caress the body's capacity for both physical skinly touch *and* metaphorical affective touch. Paterson's encounter could be said to be typically built upon the phallocentric notion of the caress, in its one-off, hotel liaisons. This seems to be a contradictory positioning given the essay's title and its intentions towards the intensities and excesses involved with touch in this 'unhomely home' (163).

Caresses, according to the dictionary, are defined as gentle touches or gestures of fondness, tenderness or love (*OED*) which locates them as intimate gestures between bodies that are already in consensual contact with one another. While caressing is perhaps primarily thought of as the erotic touch that takes place between lovers it also occurs between parent and child, child and parent as well as between friends: a caress of sympathy or support, a caress of welcome through cheek-to-cheek greeting. Thought of in this guise the caress more directly references Irigaray's caress-as-gesture, which implicates both parties as active participants.

However, the caress is also a solitary act: caressing one's self, or self-caressing, which sets the caressing body as doubled: both subject and object, active and passive.

These notions of the caress will be addressed within this chapter through taking reciprocal exchange as a key theme. Thus, while acknowledging there are varying modalities of the caress, the focus here will be upon three particular aspects: the caress as a metaphysical concept in its capacity to dissolve or even annihilate the distance between self and other; secondly as a utopian concern in that it operates as a site of mutual exchange; and thirdly, as communion between two lovers, an erotic and sensual mode of openness.

Proximity

The physical caress is a proximal activity: it involves skinly contact and anticipation of that touch ahead of itself. The notion of term 'proximity' as used by Lévinas (1969: 166), refers to an openness prior to contact or the condition upon which contact relies. For Lévinas, then, proximity operates within the broader idea of touch, beyond a model of touching–touched, referring additionally to elements of contact that exist between two separated bodies, ideas that he builds on from Aristotle's *Laws of Association* (AD 350). Feminist philosopher Cathryn Vasseleu also develops these ideas, asserting that proximity can be thought of as an 'exorbitance' and that it 'is a sensibility prior to any conscious sensation and irreducible to it' (1991: 145).

Thinking about the caress in terms of proximity or the proximal sets up a form of touch between bodies that does not necessarily involve or require physical contact, but does include it. It is out in front of contact, but also in its after effect. Paterson refers to this as 'affective touch' in his analysis of Reiki[1] therapy, but I want to suggest here that Lévinas's 'proximal' offers a broader model, one that implicates that which precedes touch, something Vasseleu also notes when she suggests that, 'for Lévinas, the body is the very advent of consciousness' (1991: 146). Looked at in this way, what Lévinas presents is an understanding of the body as an event (1978: 47).

It is desire, he proposes, that propels the self towards the object and in so doing suggests a desiring mode which seeks to be open towards the object and enter *into* relationship with it as the consenting other. In offering sensibility the caress moves beyond sensing to form a field of tactile 'exorbitance'.

Thought about in these terms, the caress becomes an unmediated encounter. For Lévinas it is 'the impossibility of reducing the other to myself, of coinciding into sameness. From an ethical perspective, two have a better time than one' (Lévinas in Cohen 1986: 22).

In resetting the relationship with another (even if that other is the self through self-touching), an event takes place in which the boundaries of each body are evaded along with the fixedness of meaning associated with them. This is an event of intimacy where the sense of self is not given up, but rather in the intimacy with the other, it becomes diffused and multiplied, a space of excess.

In the multiplicity of pre-touch, touch, affect and effect, body–mind communication becomes complicated. This blurs the distinction between perceiving and knowing, and bodily sensations become decentred. It is this site of skinly diffusion that Irigaray refers to when she considers the caress:

> It is not, therefore, in the fusion or in the ecstasy of the One that the dualism between subject and object is overcome, but rather in the incarnation of the two, a two which is irreducible to the One
>
> (IRIGARAY 2000: 59)

Proximity in these terms offers a space of openness and potential in which the self is propelled across the surface of itself. In seeking to know the unknown and unseen, the body encounters alterity and diffusion at the very boundaries of the self.

In thinking about textile as a caressing subject/object the relationships and experiences of the intimate space between body and clothing are key points of focus. It is a space of constant and intimate encounter. As the body moves and slides against and with clothing.

The caress of cloth lies somewhere between the caress of another and the self-caress; it sets the cloth as an active agent in ways that other non-human substances don't habitually take on. In the confluence of cloth's flexibility, pliability and ubiquity, it becomes part of a usual way of interacting with the world. They wrap themselves around bodies, protecting its surfaces from exposure. Cloth, in its ubiquity, becomes taken for granted and becomes invisible. While at the same time it is the most obvious of signifiers and display of self, status, mood and habitus. Wearing cloth is both to caress and be caressed.

Opening out – becoming . . .

According to Lévinas:

> what the caress seeks is not situated in a perspective and in the light of the graspable. The carnal, the tender *par excellence* correlative of the caress, the beloved, is to be identified neither with the body-thing of the physiologist, nor with the lived-body [*corps propre*] of the 'I can', nor with the body-expression, attendance its own manifestation, or face. In the caress, a relation yet in one aspect, sensible, the body already denudes itself of its very form, offering itself as erotic nudity. In carnal given to tenderness, the body quits the status of an existent.
>
> (LÉVINAS 1969: 258)

This extends the idea of the caress as a proximal relationship to focus upon the relational interplay within the structure of the skin. This sets the caress as becoming skinly, which is repeatedly brought into being at the site of the cloth and clothes covering the body.

The notion of the caress as a site of becoming skinly derives from the interplay between dermis and epidermis layers of the skin involved in touch. The skin at its most obvious is the outer covering of the body that simultaneously 'protects us from others and exposes us to them' (Cataldi 1993: 145). As such it operates as what Sara Ahmed calls 'the fleshy interface between bodies and worlds' (Ahmed and Stacey 2001: 1). In this context the skin is always in the process of becoming meaningful; it is open to being read through such signs as blushing, sweating and rashes for example.

Structurally the skin is formed of three layers: firstly the epidermis or surface of the skin, a protective layer which is constantly regenerating itself; below that is the dermis, the thickest layer, and the one responsible for the skin's pliability and mechanical resistance, but also involved in body temperature regulation, containing the sense receptors for most forms of touch, pressure and pain, blood vessels, nerve fibres, sebaceous and sweat glands and hair follicles; and lastly the subcutaneous layer, made up mostly of loose connective tissue and fat, which enables it to act as a protective cushion as well as aid insulation.

The dermis, then, is the powerhouse of the skin in terms of touch, containing sense receptors for light touch, deep pressure and vibration, pain, temperature changes and itchiness. The dermis receives and transmits information about these different forms of touch to the brain, offering a site for establishing subtle blends and changes in relation to the world.

Where the dermis is the site for reading the world, the epidermis is the site for the world's reading of the body, making it the external communicator. The other touches the epidermis and *vice versa*, while the dermis receives information about that other. In seeking a phenomenological understanding of the notion of touch, Merleau-Ponty referred to the body as 'sensible for itself' (1964: 135) and it is from within this sensibility that he derived the notion of the *chiasm* or intertwining. He illustrates this as a person clasping their hands together. As one hand grasps the other one is touched, the other touching, each with its own reversible tactile experience: touching becomes touched and *vice versa* (141). This chiasmus or intertwining involves the dermis and epidermis separating and reconnecting as the touched and touching hands reverse (141). Sartre hints at this in his description of the caress and Irigaray further develops the notion for a thinking-meaning-making female body. Somewhat less poetically the caress can be considered in terms of the dermis and epidermis, shifting from sensing the lover's skin surface or epidermis to sensing that other lover's body movements and changes through the lover's dermis. The language here becomes difficult in recognizing that both lovers are active and meaning-making participants. The chiasmus moves beyond Sartre's male lover arousing the skin of his female object of desire, and from this complication of the two lovers the caress as a model for skin-cloth interplay emerges.

The caress differs from Merleau-Ponty's touching–touched model with major implications: the caress is not that which delivers up the other as an object to be touched, rather it is a way of bringing into being that which one touches. The caress is a seeking-to-know. In Irigarayan terms 'the caress weds without consum[mat]ing . . . perfects while abiding by the outlines of the other' (1984: 186). It is this notion of wedding without consummation that acts as counterpoint to Merleau-Ponty's reversibility of touched and touching where the subject is central. For Irigaray subject over object powerplay is dismantled to offer a way of thinking that incorporates the possibility of subject–subject relationships, self-touching. Merleau-Ponty's self-touching in his discussion of his two hands touching (1945: 106), sets up a model of 'double sensations' which requires an act of will for the changing of role by the hands from subject to object. Irigaray's caress is haptic encounter in which touching necessitates mutuality. 'Everything is exchanged, yet there are no transactions ... no determinable objects . . . Our bodies are nourished by our mutual pleasure' (Irigaray and Gill 1985: 213). In this Irigaray could be accused of taking an essentialist, and potentially, utopian viewpoint with regards to capitalist structures of exchange and ownership. However, what Irigaray describes here is a way into language and expression that presents a logic that is returned to the body. This offers reciprocity rather than reversibility, or what political philosopher Hannah Arendt calls enlarged thinking:

> To think with an enlarged mentality means that one trains one's imagination to go visiting.
>
> (ARENDT 1978: 257)

Thought of in these terms, the caress offers a mode of becoming touching/touched. Within the space of the caress, an involuting gesture-space, the dermis and epidermis are activated together and separately. Irigaray's caress is expansive and occupies a space that is about two-ness. It is a generative space.

Oslo-based artist Kari Steihaug, works with used textiles that she unravels, deconstructs and uses to create large-scale installations. In the unravelling, the garments' memories take on a transience that highlights the fleeting life of many cloths and the experiences they share with the bodies they clothed. In Steihaug's work the intimacy of the cloth with the body becomes a generative space between body and cloth (Plates 21 and 22). As the fabric shifts with, and slides across, the body, so the body is constantly being touched and retouched. The relationship with clothing lies between being touched and self-touching and in this sense the erotic charge emitted could be said to be both heightened and made more tenuous. One can move consciously and purposefully to cause the clothing to come closer to its body through the action of pulling a cardigan closer, smoothing a skirt across one's legs or twirling around to feel the softness of the cloth of the kilt fall back into its folds around one's thighs and knees. On the other hand, as one goes about one's daily life, clothes, particularly the base layers of underwear, shirts and t-shirts, settle up close against the body, folding into the most intimate caress. One is only partially aware of the interplay until it is either not there any longer or it rubs, making its presence unwanted. Like the caress, the press of clothing hovers within the realm of the erotic, whose charge lies in its ambiguity and anticipation: it is both ubiquitous and particular.

Returning to Steihaug's unravelling clothing, this hovering, tenuous intimacy becomes drawn out and memories of that erotic charge are evoked, or caressed into presence, through the dispersed threads. It is in this sense that 'the caress leads each person back to the I' (Irigaray 2000a: 27). In her meditation upon the caress, *I Love to You,* Irigaray emphasizes the role of the word 'to' as directional and in the way that it draws the space between as an active partner within the relationship. Thus through the caress, 'I give you to yourself because you are a *you* for me (italics in original)' (2000: 27). In the use of 'I Love to You', she argues for a relationship that is not about possession of, or power over, the other, but about creating a space between, a space of and for proximity and enlarged thinking, between interiority and exteriority, between dermis and epidermis.

> In this double desire, 'you' and 'I' always remain active and passive, perceiving and experiencing, awake and welcoming. In us, sensible nature and the spirit become in-stance by remaining within their own singularity and grow through the risk of an exchange with what is irreducible to oneself.
> (IRIGARAY 2000a: 29)

Measuring distance

As Steihaug's clothes were once in caressing relationship with their wearers, active partners in creating the erotic charge in their relationships, so in her installations, the threads reveal Lévinas's notion of proximity as a precondition for Irigaray's caress. These (inter)relationships between body and cloth brings into being an affective and generative space of close communion. Considering these ideas and the model of the caress in terms of textile practices suggests a kind of knowledge that extends beyond language and engages directly within the body-cloth space. This intimate space operates as a site for Irigaray's 'to', from which you-ness and I-ness can emerge and expand through the interplay between them. Many of my own artworks can be considered through their capacity to establish and measure ground between dermis and epidermis. There is a suggestion of a generative space of the caress between bodies and ways in which body and cloth operate together in caressing exchange.

Printed textiles that take on a sculptural form have become an obsession and accumulation built from the repetition of the hand with cloth, a caress. As such the work offers fluidity of meaning and the potential for fertile paradoxes. They are layered, suggesting readings that extend between and beyond the interwoven ethical, political and aesthetic concerns evident within this practice. This work, with its digitally printed silk satin and silk organza layers, softly moving against one another, maintains a subtle dialect, a caressing.

In *Warp & Waft* (2016) (Plate 23) the interplay of closeness and distance becomes an invitation to the viewer. The works hover between the sculptural and performative, a triptych, but without hierarchy (Plate 24). The knitted and woven imagery emphasizes their ephemerality: neither soft nor hard, but always consumed as both. This layered ensemble, with its moiré effect offers a refusal of such consumption, presenting an intimate and proximal relationship between planes, between forms. The title *Warp & Waft* is intentionally ambiguous and draws attention to the formation of the cloth, and the ways of self-touching, of soft and hard forms across skin, emphasizing the caressing relationship between cloth and skin. The intertwining of closeness and distance draws the viewer into

TEXTILE AS CARESSING SUBJECT/OBJECT 107

the work. This work becomes a means by which to explore the discontinuities and continuities that exist in this skin-cloth relationship. The works are intended to complicate, and enfold, the viewer within this work. They offer a form of caressing practice. This metaphoric mode of practice presents a bond of generative identity and difference that emerges from the interplay between body, cloth and viewer.

These dermal layers: the outer, sensed, epidermis and the inner, sensing, dermis, occur and reoccur in *Warp & Waft* and my work more broadly. There is a display of inter-[2] and intra-dermality that is metaphorical and literal. The dermis and epidermis of my part-cloths and intimate portraits of them, the surface of the photographs and the cloths reveal and conceal narratives, skins and cloths. These elements become held together, creating interstices and gaps where identity and alterity emerge and secrete from within the layers of self-touching and self-caressing.

What could be taken to be a strategy of estrangement in *Warp & Weft* in its woven metal and knitted linen, sets up a body-cloth-self relationship as an event of creative transformation. As body, skin and cloth caress each other a space of proximity and intimacy emerges in which each participant: artist, image, cloths and viewer retains their individual 'I'ness and offers to the other their 'You'ness, creating a caress-as-gesture-space. This space of the caress brings bodies together diffusing and highlighting one another. The work produces confusion and blurs the edges of meaning such that the space becomes open to the viewer and thus Irigaray's 'non-consum(mat)ing marriage'. In foregrounding the intimacy of the cloth-skin relationship, the space of the photograph becomes affective. The other is at the surface of the image and simultaneously beyond the surface: dermis and epidermis collapse the distance between the two.

First actions of hands

The caress as gesture-word or gesture-space which 'extends beyond the distance of intimacy' (Irigaray 2000a: 26) establishes a remarkable and paradoxical model for thinking which confounds the presupposition of the intimate here and the distance there. Further, it suggests a form of what could be thought of as a primal gesture between two – a first haptic encounter with the other – which is not built upon an image, but from tactile sensation; its prehension and affect. Such a model champions the multiple: through the caress touching becomes multiple. Sensations splinter and conjoin, layering over each other and it is from among this multiplicity that the generative power of the caress emanates.

The idea of the caress as layered and multiple springs readily to mind when one first encounters the felt works of Stephanie Metz (Plate 25). These works could be said to speak of origin stories and first actions of hands – a bringing into being of bodily forms that mingle with Irigaray. Metz's work is front-loaded with its own creative process, surface and form, skin and bone. They carry a sense of progression from the subjective or intimate to the universal and back again. In this section, I want to focus upon the role of the caress-as-gesture.

On first encountering Metz's work, I was immediately caught up with their sense of primal nature. The particular work that I am referring to is the installation *Flesh & Bone* (2014) (Plate 26) comprised of hand needle-felted, bone-coloured forms. Part-bone, part-skin, the varied and various soft surfaced elements are displayed in a museum-like formation. What struck me was the consciousness of the artist's physical and metaphorical presence in these forms. The input of Metz's hands was evident in the marks of the needle repeatedly pressed into the felt as it formed the primal, bodily shapes. There is a playfulness and pleasure in their scatological associations. They have their own logic of production, which mimics bodily forms and the body's processes. This logic of production that Metz draws attention to could be considered to be a form of Irigaray's caress.

As a gesture, Irigaray's caress does not focus upon the relationship between one and another or subject and object, but rather it has at its core the relationship *between* two subjects and as such foregrounds notions of inter- and intra-subjectivity. As the one subject opens out to and onto the other subject, so that other subject returns and repeats, establishing a reciprocal relationship of exchange through touching–being touched. The caress necessitates proximity and thus unmediated contiguity between two skins which is the site of the caress's burgeoning out or an 'exorbitance'.

Metz's work brings artist, artwork and viewer into proximal and intimate relationship at the surface. In her hand-felted forms, boundaries collapse through bodily encounter. Metz's multiple shapes and forms re-emphasize bodily contact: curving and rolled spinal columns, short skeletal stacks, rib-like carapaces, skin-like panels. One 'feels' the shapes in advance of identifying or naming them, which puts the bodily and visceral out in front of the head and words. In Metz's work body to body and subject to subject communication is foregrounded: it can be felt in the hands, by the action of the arms and torso.

The hand is the first tool and through Metz's hand-felting, she highlights the relationship between hand and body, the material of her works and their forms. As needle and hand come into contact with the wool, shapes are brought into being. In a return to Irigaray's caressing lover, Metz places production of her work within the register of the body and its drives, she draws attention to art-making as an extension of the self through its body. Her work suggests space for Hannah Arendt's 'enlarged mentality' where body and mind go visiting.

Metz's work stretches and expands its own metaphors and through this understanding lies not so much in singular narratives, but in the knots or tangles within the felted forms. These knots are generative in that they bring together multiple associations and metaphors and in so doing articulate the work more coherently through the material matrix formed than each individual association. And yet, the work cannot be *explained*, it appears to hold within itself latency. This is carnal knowing' that transcends language and draws on the caress to find understanding. Such understanding can be found not in the fusion of object and subject, but in the interplay between or in the multiplicity of the caress.

Synoptic–synthaesthetic caressing

The caress, according to Irigaray, is not a call for each body to return within themselves, but rather it is the 'incarnation of the two, a two which is irreducible to the One' (Irigaray 2000a: 59). In this space of two-ness there exists at the same time the ambiguity of both synaesthesia and synopticity.

In the sense that the Irigarayan caress 'leads each person back to the *I* and to the *you* (italics in original)' (2000a: 27) it involves mingling of sensible bodies. These bodies are the vehicles for perception and expression and, moreover, within the caress each combines or pervades *with* the other. The caress demands cooperation, offering up dermis and epidermis together to each other's active and desiring co-presence. Within the caress *you*-ness and *I*-ness give out an excess or exorbitance that emerges as more than the sum of its individual parts. The *you* and *I* become expanded and cooperative fields of existence through the caress.

In describing the caress as a synoptic event or mode for expression I have drawn on Vivian Sobchack's reading of this term as 'lived as the entirety and entity that is the lived–body as access to the world and to conscious experience' (1992: 82). In the same way that the modalities of expression cooperate through the body and thus its being-in-the-world (82), so too the caress operates synoptically in that the two bodies involved cooperate through that gesture and across the proximal and mutually affective space they create. The caress takes a combined or comprehensive view of the two bodies in the world, drawing them together across and within its realm of interior and exterior modalities. Thus, a perceptual field is circumscribed around multiple points of orientation. The caress as synoptic presents or creates a corporeal system in which bodies, interior, exterior and other become a comprehensive and (temporarily) coherent system or modality or register of gestural expression. The caress as model for textile practice and theory (inter)relationships offers a system of and for expression which foregrounds the cloth-skin space as a thinking-meaning-making site across and with the body it clothes.

CONCLUSION

It is a complicated activity to talk and write about the practice of making artwork as there is an inherent danger that its non-logical elements and necessarily absurd and non-linear connections become rounded off and caged in. When doing so, it is vital to maintain the distance between theoretical and practice-based perspectives so that one is not prioritized over the other. Thus, a key aspect here has been to establish fertile ground between these two poles to highlight ways in which the practice-based and theoretical aspects function together as an interdependent relationship.

Such interdependency is affected by the way in which the various elements within the relationship are brought together, and that is why the notions of 'seaming', 'fraying' and 'folding' have emerged as the overarching organizational principles for thinking about textile practice and theory interplay. Likewise, the shimmering, the viscous and the caress speak of ways in which the elements within cloth operate in relation to each other as interdependent elements. In order to approach a set of conclusions, this final chapter will return to the topography between practice and theory and the formation of its landscape through folding, the shimmer, fraying, the viscous, seaming and the caress. These six themes, threaded together, foreground textile as an agent for bringing the material matrix into being, establishing a philosophy of textile through its modes and practice.

Thinking-through-practice

Taking these textile modes as routes for thinking-through-practice, I want to reflect briefly here on the outward-facing aspects of textile practices, most commonly as exhibited artworks. Conscious of the warnings here, I am interested in establishing a strategy that develops a philosophy of practice through the very processes that that practice is engaged with. In this way, it is possible to sidestep, or borderswerve, the cage and flow freely within and between textile practice and theory. From a practice-focused perspective staging an exhibition or performance marks a point of consolidation and reflection upon the practice–theory interplay holistically. It is also an opportunity to stand away from the immediacy of both material practice processes and theoretical perspectives. In this sense making the work public offers a point for reflection upon the aims and its potential through extended understanding of the relationships between perception and materiality.

In curating an exhibition, performance or installation of artworks, the interconnectivity between each element or work can become clearer, not necessarily in the sense of a narrative or prescriptive journey through the works, but in terms of the logic that allows for paths through the enfolded and enfolding practice. In this sense seaming, folding and fraying become curatorial strategies for selecting and piecing the work together using the repertoire of textile techniques

Inevitably there are works or elements not selected, curatorial decisions being made to maintain aesthetic and conceptual consistency between the works exhibited and also to avoid repetition or overcrowding of the space. These elements act as nodes or points of intersection on the material matrix of textile practice–theory considerations.

Textile practices as methodology

In seeking to capitalize upon the rich language associated with textile practice, production, behaviour and materiality, one of the aims has been to extend the role of textile within broader discourses of practice. This is a textile-based methodology that emerges from within the textile practices and processes. These are modes of thinking that are embedded within the processes, histories, theories and vocabulary of textile. These methodologies function together not just to gather and process information, but also as modes of articulation. I use this word both in terms of its writing and speaking sense, but also in the sense of the way the different aspects of the research material and findings are jointed or brought together: they juxtapose and overlap each other, their porous edges fraying and frayed at the point of encounter.

Fraying has been highlighted here as an organizing principle for textile practice not only for the way it offers a mode for bringing theoretical information and perspectives together, or enabling the textile practice–theory (inter)relationship to flourish, but also for embedding and connecting practice-based aspects. Where Sarat Maharaj refers to Janis Jefferies' practice–theory relationship as 'The drenched–in–voice quality of [her] *think–speak–write* sequences, their soaked-in-oral feel signals the pivotal element of her expression – unscriptedness' (Maharaj in Mitchell 2000: 8), he highlights speaking, making and writing interplay as frayed, fraying and porous modes of expression. Fraying here offers something similar, and in consciously drawing upon textile-rooted language it actively highlights the specifics that such a textile-based process refers to in terms of both form and function, while also opening the idea up metaphorically, seeking that 'drenched-in'

CONCLUSION

quality of Jefferies' writing practice. The notion of fraying, then, not only considers the edges or revealing of structural elements, but also emphasizes the manner and process of that unweaving. The frayed edge or worn centre makes space for, and utilizes, the raw edges that become revealed as mechanisms and/or processes. To think of fraying as a methodological mode for the interplay between practice and theory recognizes the need for both porosity and uncertainty to occur at the edges and worn centres such that meaning and understanding can cross and slip between modes of practice. In this it offers a porous and mingling space of exchange across textile practice–theory (inter)relationships.

In terms of textile practice as a methodology, the processes and behaviours discussed demonstrate that affectivity and relational interplay does not necessarily take simultaneous nor linear routes. As cloth moves, stretches and is joined, it offers new ways for communicating textile practices.

The themes or models of the 'behavioural' chapters operate in partnership with textile processes. Textile as a Shimmering Landscape (Chapter 2) suggests a form in which flickering within and between the warp–weft, light–dark relationships open up and reveal textile structures. Shimmering is often most obvious at the site of the fold where the cloth bends back on itself and its surfaces catch the light. Textile as Viscous Substance (Chapter 4) sets the relationship between practice and theory as a more viscous form in which the worn and thinned centre reveals the sticky residues that hold the cloth in place before complete disintegration. Raw and fraying edges, brought together with other raw edges offers a model that enables the particular qualities of each element or fabric to be retained and referenced within the viscous mix and again it can be seen that structure and behaviour function together. Additionally, the fraying edge suggests a space for the transfer of information to move freely across and between the two fabrics, suggesting a mode that echoes the viscous as a model for practice–theory (inter) relationships. Textile as Caressing Subject/Object (Chapter 6) focuses upon the interplay between epidermis and dermis within the caress as a mode of touching, mirroring the relational interplay between warp and weft within cloth. The relationship that emerges between in this chapter can be regarded as a form of seaming in that as subject caresses another subject the two subjects' epidermises and dermises come up against each other without consumption or possession, while retaining their own autonomy within the caressing–seaming exchange and enabling an articulation of both in conjunction with one another through these layers and joinings.

Textile practices as a methodological model for textile practice–theory interplay operate within a much broader sense here as it brings elements of practice and theory together. Thinking in terms of the theoretical foci that have emerged, it is by bringing them together in relationship with each other that makes these modes of thinking-through-practice reveal their potency, creating new pools of thinking and understanding about practice–theory (inter)relationships. Using textile practices, at its edges and centres, the varied approaches: philosophical, phenomenological, psychoanalytical, textile, feminist and post-structuralist come together and alongside one another to enable creative exchange.

As Deleuze and Guattari's philosophical model of smooth and striated space (Deleuze and Guattari 1980: 538) comes up against textile structures and language, it becomes clear that this is a site of fraying and pooling where the structural elements are revealed and exchange is enabled. This is not so much Maharaj's 'art–engineering' (Mitchell 2000: 8) but a fluid or plastic mode of communication. In this textile practice offers up an extension to Deleuze and Guattari's model of woven cloth as striated, suggesting it as a model for flows and intensities between smooth and striated. Sometimes cloth operates as 'pure' striated, bounded, linear space such as when it is held taut on the loom or stiffened and sometimes operates as 'pure' smooth space, where there is flow and infinitude and the warp and weft fray, allowing more freedom in relation to each other. More often, however, woven cloth operates within and between smooth and striated, shimmering across the frayed edge and worn centre.

Similarly, Kristeva's notion of the abject and abjection, when considered in relation to the viscosity of napped cloths such as velvet offers seaming and joining. Where the napped surface of velvet for some offers the sensation of luxuriousness and opulence and they revel in caressing its surface, for others the cloth's skin-like surface provokes a physical response of revulsion, making the skin want to shrink away from the cloth. In this, three different elements of thinking-through-practice are brought together: textile as metaphor for skin, the caress as interplay between dermis and epidermis, and the psychoanalytical theories of abjection and threatened borders. Here the seam draws together and mixes all three to produce a complex and mobile surface or structure that references boundaries and borders in a mirroring of the concepts of desire and abjection. Within this structure, the pile of the velvet marks the direction of the weave structure as it catches the light across the surface of the seam, momentarily disrupting movement across that surface, but also enabling the change of plane through the articulation of that seaming.

Practice–theory interplay

The twists and turns that any practice, set as a mode of thinking has to negotiate are sometimes difficult to identify until it is well developed and the terrain or landscape becomes clearer as the view extends beyond the immediacy of the pathway. Nowhere would this be more so than in thinking about practice–theory where (at least) two modes of coming-to-know offer different approaches to knowledge acquisition and, vitally, different understandings of what that knowledge might be.

CONCLUSION

Through focusing upon thinking-through-practice, the relationship between warp and weft within woven cloth has been offered as a model for textile practice–theory relationships. Textile practice resides within and between fine art, craft and applied art discourses. The different processes and behaviours discussed here highlight and develop thinking about, and through, textile both as an active agent and site for bringing the borderlines between these discourses into focus. At and on these borderlines[5] understandings drawn from textile-based knowledge regarding the structure and behaviour of woven cloth can come together with other modes of thinking as a model to further enhance understanding of both. Additionally, and this is a crucial point here, such a model offers the relationships within the material matrix of textile, textile language and textile production, as more subtle and nuanced developments. This then suggests a materialization for Deleuze and Guattari's model of striated and smooth, not in the sense of spaces that operate in utopian purity, but rather as folded together with each other in intensities and flows.

Thinking of the relationship between practice-based and theoretical concerns as a form of folding that seeks to enable the transfer of language, understanding and knowledge across the borderlines between practice and theory, opens up the possibility of a model which actively considers the folds of cloth, the points of inflection created and also the mechanism or process by which that folding (and the implications of unfolding and enfolding) occurs. These can be metaphorical foldings, practice-based enwrappings or indeed modes of textile-writing which actively and consciously demonstrate folded and folding forms of thinking–speaking–writing textile. It is from within such a triadic model of textile practice that the strength of folding as an organizing mode for bringing into being the material matrix of practice–theory thinking and making becomes highlighted in its ability to bring together warp–weft (inter)relationships within one aspect with the warp–weft (inter)relationships with another in a variety of interdependent ways.

In terms of the title, *A Philosophy of Textile* and the ideas which initiated this exploration of textile-based(inter) relationships, folding offers up an organizing principle which prioritizes the interplay between textile practice and theory as modes for thinking. The apparent simplicity of the idea of folding: the process of doubling over a piece of fabric belies the complexity of folding, unfolding and enfolding formed in that process. In this sense, then 'folding' offers an ongoing mode for identifying spaces that enable and reveal practice–theory operating together.

In bringing together the materiality, imagery and language of textile here, to think through and across modes of thinking, making and writing, I am aware of the contingency involved. This, then, is not a conclusion, but perhaps a looping back to another place on the matrix of knowing. Textile practice and theory are mobile and mutable concepts, they intertwine and generate meaning within their (inter)relationships. For the textile practitioner, this book is offered as a way for thinking-through-making: writing textile, making text.

NOTES

Introduction

1 Charles Sanders Peirce (1839–1914) formulated a triadic model of the sign, which included the representamen, the object and the intrepretant. According to his theory, the way in which we interpret a sign is what gives it its meaning.

Chapter 2

1 Irmin's installation is a grid-like maze of sixteen rectangular chambers, each formed from white scrim panels with a vertical fluorescent tube on each wall. The tubes are wrapped with colour gels in sections, identical in each room, but the patterns change between rooms. As the viewer looks down the length of the chambers, a view of repeated openings and tubes, each framing the next, can bet seen, repeated squares and part-squares, lights and screens, creating an almost mirror-like sense of perspective.

2 Cixous did in fact wear glasses before the operation to rectify her myopia and this text highlights the way in which, in her previous existence, she was able to play around with what and how she saw/viewed the world about her, something that became lost to her post-operatively.

3 All quotations here refer to the reprinted version in *Desire in Language* (1980: 64–91).

4 Alissa Auther provides a fuller discussion and analysis of these movements in *String, Felt, Thread* (2009).

5 This exhibition was the result of new research by Hesse scholar Professor Briony Fer and was curated by Fer together with Barry Rosen, Director of The Estate of Eva Hesse. Fer collectively renamed these objects as 'studioworks' (Fer 2009), proposing that their precarious nature places them at the heart of Hesse's work and questions traditional notions of what sculpture is.

Chapter 3

1 Artist statement: http://www.annhamiltonstudio.com/videosound/follow.html (accessed 27 August 2013).

Chapter 4

1. Conversation with the artist in Birmingham, 21 January 2012.
2. Conversation with the artist in Birmingham, 21 January 2012.
3. Curator's talk in Birmingham, 21 January 2012.

Chapter 5

1. In psychoanalytic terms, cathexis refers to the libidinal energy invested in some ideas or person or object (*OED*). Thus, cathexis is a form of emotional investment transferred into an object to form a link between the self and the outside world.

Chapter 6

1. Reiki is a method of stress reduction and relaxation that also promotes healing through the transferral of bodily energies. The technique was developed in Japan and is administered by the laying on of hands.
2. The prefix *inter-* means between or among, while *intra-* means within, so here I want to highlight the caress as a form of expression of subjectivity both between sensing subjects and within the one sensing subject (i.e. as in self-touching).

BIBLIOGRAPHY

Agamben, G. 'What Is a Paradigm?' Lecture given at the European Graduate School, Switzerland, 2002.
Ahmed, S. and J. Stacey. *Thinking Through the Skin*. London: Routledge, 2001.
Anderson, K. 'Ecstatic Subjects, Utopia, and Recognition: Kristeva, Heidegger, Irigaray'. *The Journal of Utopian Studies* 11 (2000): 170–2.
Archer, N. 'Text(Ile)s: How to Fabric(Ate) Yourself a Body without Organs'. *Textile: The Journal of Cloth and Culture* 2, no. 2 (2004): 156–75. https://doi.org/10.2752/1 47597504778052748.
Arendt, H. *The Life of the Mind: Thinking*, Vols 1 and 2. San Diego: Harcourt Publishers Ltd, 1978. Aristotle, 350AD. De Anima (On the Soul), 1987th ed. London: Penguin Classics.
Asbury, M. *Anna Maria Maiolino*. London: Camden Arts Centre, 2010.
Auther, E. *String, Felt, Thread: The Hierarchy of Art and Craft in American Art*. Minneapolis: University of Minnesota Press, 2009.
Ayers, R. 'Everywhere and Nowhere: Robert Ayers in Conversation with Ann Hamilton'. A Sky Filled with Shooting Stars, 2009.
Bachmann, I. and S. Ruth (eds). *Material Matters: The Art and Culture of Contemporary Textiles*. Toronto: YYZBooks, 1998.
Bal, M. *Louise Bourgeois' 'Spider': The Architecture of Art-Writing*. Chicago: University of Chicago Press, 2001.
Barnett, P. (ed.). *Textures of Memory: The Poetics of Cloth*. Nottingham: Angel Row Gallery, 1999.
Barrette, B. *Eva Hesse: Sculpture*. New York: Rizzoli International Publications, 1989.
Barthes, R. *Camera Lucida: Reflections on Photography*. New York: Hill and Wang, 1981.
Barthes, R. *A Lover's Discourse: Fragments*, 2002nd edn. London: Cape, 1979.
Barthes, R. *The Neutral: Lecture Course at the Collège De France, 1977–1978*. New York: Columbia University Press, 1978.
Barthes, R. *Image, Music, Text*. London: Fontana, 1977.
Barthes, R. *The Pleasure of the Text*. New York: Hill and Wang, 1973.
Benjamin, W. *The Arcades Project*. Cambridge, MA: Belknap Press, 1999.
Benjamin, W. *The Origin of German Tragic Drama*. London: NLB, 1977.
Benjamin, W. *Illuminations*, 1999th edn. London: Pimlico, 1936.
Bishop, Claire (ed.). *Participation. Documents of Contemporary Art*. London: Whitechapel Gallery, 2006.
Bishop, Claire. *Installation Art a Critical History*. London: Tate Publishing, 2005.
Bochner, Mel. 'The Serial Attitudes'. *Artforum International* 6 (December 1967): 28.
Bolt, B. *Art beyond Representation: The Performative Power of the Image*. London: I.B. Tauris, 2004.

Borges, J. L. *A Universal History of Infamy*, New edn. Harmondsworth: Penguin Books Ltd, 1946.
Bourgeois, L. *Louise Bourgeois*. London: Tate Gallery Publications, 2000.
Braidotti, R. *Metamorphoses: Towards a Materialist Theory of Becoming*. Cambridge: Polity & Blackwells, 2002.
Bruno, G. *Surface: Matters of Aesthetics, Materiality, and Media*. Chicago and London: University of Chicago Press, 2014.
Bryan-Wilson, Julia. *Fray Art and Textile Politics*. Chicago: University of Chicago Press, 2017.
Bryant, A. and G. Pollock. *Digital and Other Virtualities: Renegotiating the Image*. London: I.B. Tauris, 2010.
Buszek, M. E. *Extra/Ordinary: Craft and Contemporary Art*. Durham, N.C.: Duke University Press, 2011.
Calvino, I. and W. Weaver. *Invisible Cities*, 1975th edn. London: Secker and Warburg, 1972.
Carter, P. *Material Thinking: The Theory and Practice of Creative Research*. Melbourne: Melbourne University Press, 2004.
Cataldi, S. L. *Emotion, Depth and Flesh: A Study of Sensitive Space - Reflections on Merleau- Ponty's Philosophy of Embodiment*. New York: State University of New York Press, 1993.
Certeau, Michel de. *The Practice of Everyday Life*. Berkeley: University of California Press, 1984.
Cixous, H. *Stigmata: Escaping Texts*, 2005th edn. London: Routledge, 1998.
Cixous, H. 'The Laugh of the Medusa'. *Signs* 1 (1976): 875–93.
Cixous, H. and J. Derrida. *Veils*. Stanford: Stanford University Press, 2001.
Cohen, R. A. *Face to Face with Levinas*. Albany: State University of New York Press, 1986.
Conner, J. 'Pipilotti Rist: Rooms With Many Views'. *Interview Magazine*, 2009.
Corby, V. *Eva Hesse: Longing, Belonging and Displacement*. London and New York: I.B. Tauris, 2010.
Danchev, A. *100 Artists' Manifestos: [From the Futurists to the Stuckists]*. London: Penguin Books, 2011.
De' Marinis, F. (ed.). *Velvet: History, Techniques, Fashions*. Milan: Idea Books, 1993.
Deleuze, G. *Cinema 2: The Time-Image*. London: Continuum, 1989.
Deleuze, G. *The Fold: Leibniz and the Baroque*, 1993rd edn. London: Athlone Press, 1988.
Deleuze, G. *Difference and Repetition*, 1994th edn. London: Athlone Press, 1968.
Deleuze, G. *Proust and Signs*, 2008th edn. London: Continuum, 1964.
Deleuze, G. and F. Guattari. *A Thousand Plateaus: Capitalism and Schizophrenia*, 2004th edn. London: Continuum, 1980.
Derrida, J. *Positions*. London: T&T Clark Ltd, 2004.
Derrida, J. *Memoirs of the Blind: The Self-portrait and Other Ruins*. Chicago: University of Chicago Press, 1990.
Dickinson, Emily and Thomas H. Johnson. *Complete Poems*, New edn. London: Faber & Faber, 1976.
Douglas, M. *Purity and Danger: An Analysis of the Concepts of Pollution and Taboo*, 1991st edn. London: Routledge, 1966.
Duffy, Carol Ann. *The Bees*. London: Picador, 2012.
Eisenstein, S. *The Film Sense*, New edn. London: Faber and Faber, 1947.
Ettinger, B. *The Matrixial Borderspace*. Minneapolis: University of Minnesota Press, 2006.
Ettinger, B. 'Matrix and Metramorphosis'. *Differences: A Journal of Feminist Cultural Studies* 4 (1992): 176–208.

BIBLIOGRAPHY

Fer, B. *Precarious Fields*. London: Camden Arts Centre, 2010.
Fer, B. *Eva Hesse: Studiowork*. Edinburgh: Fruitmarket Gallery, 2009.
Foucault, M. *History of Madness*, 2006th edn. London: Routledge, 1972.
Frank, R. and G. Watson (eds). *Textiles - Open Letter*. Berlin: Sternberg Press, 2015.
Freud, Sigmund. *New Introductory Letters on Psycho-Analysis.* London: Hogarth Press, 1933.
Freud, S. *The Complete Psychological Works of Sigmund Freud - Volume 16: 'Introductory Lectures on Psycho-analysis, Part 3'*, 2001st edn. London: Vintage Classics, 1917.
Gasché, R. *The Tain of the Mirror: Derrida and the Philosophy of Reflection*. Cambridge, MA: Harvard University Press, 1986.
Gaßner, H., B. Kölle, and P. Roettig (eds). *Eva Hesse: One More than One* [... anlässlich der Ausstellung "Eva Hesse. One More than One", Hamburger Kunsthalle, 29. November 2013–02. März 2014]. Ostfildern: Hatje Cantz, 2013.
Gebauer, G. and C. Wulf. *Mimesis: Culture, Art, Society*, 1995th edn. Berkeley: University of California Press, 1992.
Gill, C. B. (ed.). *Time and the Image*. Manchester: Manchester University Press, 2000.
Hall, S. and S. Maharaj. *Annotations: Modernity and Difference No. 6*. London: Institute of International Visual Arts, 2001.
Hamilton, Ann. *Ann Hamilton: Present-Past 1984-1997*. Edited by Anna Albano. Milan: Skira, 1999.
Hamlyn, A. 'Freud, Fabric, Fetish'. *Textile: The Journal of Cloth and Culture* 1 (2003): 8–26. https://doi. org/10.2752/147597503778053117
Haraway, D. 'Situated Knowledges: The Science Question in Feminism and the Privilege of Partial Perspective'. *Feminist Studies* 14 (1988): 575–99.
Harper, Catherine. *Textiles: Critical and Primary Sources*. Oxford: Berg, 2012.
Heidegger, M. *Basic Writings: From Being and Time (1927) to The Task of Thinking (1964)*, rev. edn. London: Routledge, 1993.
Hemmings, Jessica (ed.). *Cultural Threads: Transnational Textiles Today*. London: Bloomsbury Academic, 2015.
Hemmings, Jessica. *Warp and Weft: Woven Textiles in Fashion, Art and Interiors*. London: Bloomsbury Publishing, 2012a.
Hemmings, Jessica. *The Textile Reader*. Edited by Jessica Hemmings. Berg Publishers, 2012b.
Hicks, S. *Sheila Hicks: Weaving as Metaphor*. New Haven and London: Published for the Bard Graduate Center for Studies in the Decorative Arts, Design, and Culture, New York by Yale University Press, 2006.
Hume, G. *Parkett, Gary Hume, Gabriel Orozco, Pipilotti Rist*. Zürich: Parkett-Verlag, 1996.
Huntington, P. 'Between the Scylla of Discursivity and the Charybdis of Pantextualism'. *Human Studies* 21 (1998): 197–206.
Irigaray, L. *To Be Two*. London: Athlone Press, 2000a.
Irigaray, L. *Democracy Begins Between Two*. London: Athlone Press, 2000b.
Irigaray, L. *An Ethics of Sexual Difference*, 2004th edn. London and New York: Continuum, 1993.
Irigaray, L. *Marine Lover of Friedrich Nietzsche*. Columbia: Columbia University Press, 1991.
Irigaray, L. *To Speak Is Never Neutral*, 2002nd edn. London: Continuum, 1985.
Irigaray, L. *An Ethics of Sexual Difference*, 2004th edn. London: Athlone Press, 1984.

Irigaray, L. *This Sex Which Is Not One*. Translated by Burke Porter, 1985th edn. Ithaca: Cornell University Press, 1977.
Irigaray, L. and G. C. Gill. *Speculum of the Other Woman*. Ithaca: Cornell University Press, 1985.
Irigaray, L. and M. Whitford. *The Irigaray Reader*. Oxford: Basil Blackwell, 1991.
Jakobson, R. *Fundamentals of Language*. Translated by Morris Halle. Gravenhage: Mouton & Co, 1956.
Jefferies, J. (ed.). *Reinventing Textiles*. Winchester: Telos, 2001.
Jefferies, J., D. Wood Conroy, and H. Clark. *The Handbook of Textile Culture*. London: Bloomsbury Academic, 2016.
Johnson, P. *Ideas in the Making: Practice in Theory*. London: Crafts Council, 1998.
Jones, A. *Self/Image: Technology, Representation, and the Contemporary Subject*. London: Routledge, 2006.
Jones, A. R. and P. Stallybrass. *Renaissance Clothing and the Materials of Memory*. Cambridge, England and New York: Cambridge University Press, 2001.
Jones, R. *Irigaray*. Stafford, Queensland: Polity, 2011.
Karim, A. *Dacca: The Mughal Capital*. Islamabad: Asiatic Society of Pakistan, 1964.
Kelly, M. *Post-Partum Document*. London and Boston: Routledge & Kegan Paul, 1983.
Klein, M. *Envy and Gratitude A Study of Unconscious Sources*. London: Tavistock Publications, 1957.
Krauss, R. E. 'Video: The Aesthetics of Narcissism'. *October* 1 (1976): 50–64.
Kristeva, J. *Powers of Horror: An Essay on Abjection*. New York: Columbia University Press, 1982.
Kristeva, J. *Desire in Language: A Semiotic Approach to Literature and Art*. New York: Columbia University Press, 1980.
Lacan, J. *Feminine Sexuality*. London: Palgrave Macmillan, 1982.
Lacan, J. *Écrits: A Selection*, 2001st edn. London: Routledge, 1966.
Lacoue-Labarthe, P. and C. Fynsk. *Typography: Mimesis, Philosophy, Politics*. Stanford: Stanford University Press, 1989.
Landi, A. and A. Landi. '"Jane Lackey: Enveloping Space: Walk, Trace, Think" at Center for Contemporary Arts'. *ARTnews.Com* (blog), 30 July 2014. https://www.artnews.com/art-news/reviews/jane-lackey-enveloping-space-walk-trace-think-2546/.
Leader, D. 'Minimalism with a Human Face'. *Tate Magazine* 2 (2002): 78–81.
Lechte, J. *Julia Kristeva*. London and New York: Routledge, 1990.
Lee, J. Y. 'Art Crit: Words in Images - Ann Hamilton [WWW Document]'. *What Weekly*. http://whatweekly.com/2013/11/21/words-in-images/ (accessed 1 September 2015).
Lee, P. 'Eva Hesse: San Francisco Museum of Modern Art - Reviews [WWW Document]', 2002. http://findarticles.com/p/articles/mi_m0268/is_9_40/ai_86647185/ (accessed 9 October 2010).
Lévinas, E. *Existence and Existents*. The Hague: Martinus Nijhoff, 1978.
Lévinas, E. [Totalité Et Infini.] *Totality and Infinity. An Essay on Exteriority …* Translated by Alphonso Lingis. Pittsburgh: Duquesne University Press, 1969.
Levi-Strauss, C. *Introduction to the Work of Marcel Mauss*, 1987th edn. London: Routledge & Kegan Paul, 1950.
LeWitt, S. 'Sentences on Conceptual Art'. Art-Language (1969).
LeWitt, S. 'Paragraphs on Conceptual Art'. *Artforum International* 5 (1967): 79–83.
Lippard, L. R. *Eva Hesse*. Boston: Da Capo Press, 1976.
Livingstone, Joan and John Ploof (eds) *The Object of Labor: Art, Cloth, and Cultural Production*. Cambridge, MA: MIT, 2007.

BIBLIOGRAPHY

MacCormack, P. 'Becoming Vulva: Flesh, Fold, Infinity'. *New Formations*, 68 (2009): 93–107.
Macleod, K. 'The Functions of the Written Text in Practice-Based PhD Submissions'. Working Papers in Art & Design 1, 2000.
Mangini, E. 'Pipilotti's Pickle: Making Meaning from the Feminine Position'. *PAJ: A Journal of Performance and Art* 23 (2001): 1–9.
Marchand, S. *Tricia Middleton, Dark Souls*. Montreal: Musée d'art contemporain de Montréal, 2009.
Marks, L. U. *The Skin of the Film: Intercultural Cinema, Embodiment, and the Senses*. Durham: Duke University Press, 1999.
Melberg, A. *Theories of Mimesis*. Cambridge: Cambridge University Press, 1995.
Merleau-Ponty, M. *The Primacy of Perception, and Other Essays on Phenomenological Psychology, the Philosophy of Art, History and Politics*. Edited by James M. Edie. Evanston: Northwestern University Press, 1964a.
Merleau-Ponty, M. *The Visible and the Invisible*, 1968th edn. Evanston: Northwestern University Press, 1964b.
Merleau-Ponty, M. *Phenomenology of Perception*, 1976th edn. London: Routledge & K. Paul, 1945.
Millar, L. (ed.). *Lost in Lace*. Birmingham: Birmingham Museum & Art Gallery, 2011.
Miller, N. K. *The Poetics of Gender*. New York: Columbia University Press, 1986.
Milner, M. *On not Being able to Paint*. London: William Heinemann, 1950.
Minh-ha, T. T. *When the Moon Waxes Red: Representation, Gender and Cultural Politics*, 1st edn. New York: Routledge, 1992.
Mitchell, V. 'Dialog Stitching with Metonymy'. *Textile: The Journal of Cloth and Culture* 11, no. 3 (1 November 2013): 314–19.
Mitchell, V. *Selvedges: Janis Jefferies - Works since 1980*. Norwich: Norwich School of Art & Design, 2000.
Monem, N. K. *Contemporary Textiles: The Fabric of Fine Art*. London: Black Dog, 2008.
Moore, J. *Tricia Middleton* [The Woods. CENTRE DES ARTS ACTUELS SKOL. MONTREAL]. Canadian Art, 2005.
Morris III, Charles E. *Remembering the AIDS Quilt*. East Lansing: Michigan State University Press, 2011.
Munroe, A. and I. Nakagawa. *The Third Mind: American Artists Contemplate Asia 1860–1989: American Artists Contemplate Asia 1960–1969*, 1 edn. NewYork: Guggenheim Museum Publications, 2009.
Naficy, H. (ed.). *Home, Exile, Homeland: Film, Media, and the Politics of Place*. New York: Routledge, 1999.
Nesbitt, J. (ed.). *Mneme Ann Hamilton*. London: Tate Gallery Publications, 1994.
Nixon, M. *Eva Hesse*. Cambridge, MA: MIT Press, 2002.
Pajaczkowska, C. 'Thread of Attachment'. *Textile: The Journal of Cloth and Culture* 5 (2007): 140–53.
Pajaczkowska, C. 'On Stuff and Nonsense: The Complexity of Cloth'. *Textile: The Journal of Cloth and Culture* 3, no. 3 (2005): 220–49. https://doi.org/10.2752/1 47597505778052495.
Parker, R. *The Subversive Stitch: Embroidery and the Making of the Feminine*. England: I.B. Tauris & Co, 2010.
Paterson, M. 'Caresses, Excesses, Intimacies and Estrangements'. *Angelaki: Journal of the Theoretical Humanities* 9 (2004): 165. https://doi.org/10.1080/0969725042000232478
Pejic, B. 'Maja Bajevic: The Matrix of Memory'. *Textile: The Journal of Cloth and Culture* 5 (2007): 66–87. https://doi.org/10.2752/147597507780338916

Pellicer, R. *Photomaton. Editions de la Martinière*. Paris: Martiniere, BL, 2011.
Phelan, P. (ed.). *Pipilotti Rist*. London: Phaidon, 2001.
Perreault, J. *Writing Selves Contemporary Feminist Autography*. Minneapolis: University of Minnesota Press, 1995.
Picard, C. 'Center Field - Threading Infrastructure: An Interview with Anne Wilson'. *ART21 Magazine*, 2011.
Plant, S. 1998. *Zeros + Ones: Digital Women + the New Technoculture*. London: Fourth Estate.
Polanyi, M. (1966) Polanyi, Michael. *The Tacit Dimension*. New York: Doubleday, 1966 [1st ed.]. Garden City, N.Y.: Doubleday.
Rideal, L. 'Drapery and Pattern in Portrait Painting as a Source for My Work in the Photobooth, with Particular Reference to "The Curtain Master" William Larkin'. *Textile: The Journal of Cloth and Culture* 1 (2003): 274–87.
Rideal, L., N. Bryson, and C. Darwent. *Liz Rideal: Stills*. New York: Lucas Schoormans, 2001.
Robertson, K. 'Resistance and Submission, Warp and Weft: Unraveling the Life of Ethel Mairet'. *Textile: The Journal of Cloth and Culture* 3 (2005): 292–317. https://doi.org/10.2752/147597505778052486
Robinson, H. *Reading Art, Reading Irigaray: The Politics of Art by Women*. London: I.B. Tauris, 2006.
Rosenthal, S. *Pipilotti Rist: Eyeball Massage*. London: Hayward Gallery Publishing, 2011.
Sartre, J.-P. *Being and Nothingness: An Essay on Phenomenological Ontology*, 2003rd edn. London: Routledge, 1943.
Sartre, J.-P. *Nausea*. London: Penguin, 1938.
Saussure, F. de. *Course in General Linguistics*, 1998th edn. London: Gerald Duckworth & Co Ltd, 1983.
Serres, M. *The Five Senses: A Philosophy of Mingled Bodies*, 2008th edn. London: Continuum, 1985.
Serres, M. *The Troubadour of Knowledge*. Ann Arbor: The University of Michigan Press, 1997.
Showalter, E. *The New Feminist Criticism: Essays on Women, Literature and Theory*. New York: Random House USA Inc, 1988.
Smith, T. 'Three Figures, Three Patterns, Three Paradigms [WWW Document]'. *Art Practical*. http://www.artpractical.com/feature/three-figures-three-patterns-three-paradigms/ (accessed 12 January 2017).
Smith, T. L. *Bauhaus Weaving Theory: From Feminine Craft to Mode of Design*. Minneapolis and London: University of Minnesota Press, 2014.
Sobchack, V. C. *The Address of the Eye: A Phenomenology of Film Experience*. Princeton: Princeton University Press, 1992.
Sonnenberg, R. 'Louise Bourgeois: Stitching Salvation'. *Fiberarts* 36 (2006): 36–9.
Sontag, S. *Against Interpretation: And Other Essays*, 1990th edn. New York and London: Anchor Books, Doubleday, 1966.
Sorkin, Jenni. 'Stain: On Cloth, Stigma, and Shame'. *Third Text* 14, no. 53 (2000): 77–80. https://doi.org/10.1080/09528820108576884.
Spivak, G. C. *Outside in the Teaching Machine*. London: Routledge, 1993.
Stewart, S. *On Longing: Narratives of the Miniature, the Gigantic, the Souvenir, the Collection*. Durham: Duke University Press, 1993.
Sullivan, A. *Virtually Normal: An Argument about Homosexuality*. London: Picador, 1995.
Sussman, E. *Eva Hesse: Sculpture*. New Haven: Yale University Press, 2006.

BIBLIOGRAPHY

Ullrich, E. 'Various Types of Moire Effects and Their Production'. *The Melliand*, 1, no. 8 (1930): 1205–8.
Vasseleu, C. 'The Face before the Mirror-Stage'. *Hypatia* 6 (1991): 140–55.
Vervoordt, A. *Tra: Edge of Becoming*. MER Paper Kunsthalle, 2011.
Vicuña, C. *Precario/Precarious*. New York: Tanam Press, 1983.
Vidler, A. *The Activist Drawing: Retracing Situationist Architectures from Constant's New Babylon to Beyond*. Edited by M. Catherine de Zegher and Mark Wigley. Cambridge, MA: MIT Press, 1999.
Virilio, P. and J. Rose. *A Landscape of Events*. Cambridge, MA and London: MIT, 2000.
Watson, G. 'Mona Hatoum'. *Audio Arts Magazine* 13 (1993).
Winnicott, D. 'Transitional Objects and Transitional Phenomena—A Study of the First Not-Me Possession'. *International Journal of Psychoanalysis* 34 (1953): 89–97.
Wyschogrod, E. 'Empathy and Sympathy as Tactile Encounter'. *Journal of Medicine and Philosophy* 6 (1981): 25–44. https://doi.org/10.1093/jmp/6.1.25

INDEX

Abakanowicz, Magdalena   32
Abramovic, Marina   78
absence   26–8, 53
absurd   6, 26, 31, 34–7, 60, 111
accrete   19, 36, 54, 69–70
Agamben, Giorgio   30
agency   21, 27, 44, 57, 59–60,
    62–3, 87, 95
Ahmed, Sara   58, 103
ambivalence   2, 73, 77, 91
animate   13–14, 36, 76–7, 91,
    95, 97
anxiety   9, 77, 86
arabesque   5, 14
Archer, Nicole   2
Arendt, Hannah   105, 108
Aristotle   8, 101
arouse   3, 99, 104
assemblage   21, 37, 94–7
assimilate   43, 59, 83, 93
Augustine   55
Auther, Elissa   2, 31, 34–5, 117
autography   42–3
awakening   54, 100
Ayers, Robert   55

Bachmann, Ingrid   43
backstitch   46
baffle   30, 33, 36, 39
Barnett, Pennina   2, 14, 20
Baroque   5, 12, 14–15, 22–3,
    37, 95

Barthes, Roland   3–6, 9, 25–34,
    47–9, 69, 75, 87, 92
becoming   13–16, 44, 77, 81, 97,
    103, 105
belonging   89–90
Benjamin, Walter   26, 47, 59–60, 62
Bishop, Claire   61
Bochner, Mel   35
Borges, Jorge Luis   53
boundary   26–37, 41–3, 53, 60,
    62–77, 81–95, 102, 108, 114
Bourgeois   48, 78
Braidotti, Rosi   77
Bruno, Guiliana   2, 7, 27, 53
Bryant, Antony   9
Bryan-Wilson, Julia   2, 7, 81–2, 84–5
Buszek, Maria Elena   41
button   50, 73–4

Calvino, Italo   60
capitalism   37–8, 73, 105
care   17, 21, 46, 71, 82, 94
Carter, Paul   92
categorization   33, 38, 72
cathexis   87, 118
chaos   35–6
chiasm   104
chora   48–9, 63, 76
chronology   11, 23, 63
cinema   51
Cixous, Hélène   25–38, 44–63,
    78, 81–4

INDEX

complicate 4, 69, 102, 104, 107, 111
conceal 51, 53, 68, 107
consume 38, 71, 74, 104, 106, 113
contingent 37, 58, 74, 81, 85, 90, 92, 94, 97, 115
cotton 45, 66, 68, 70
craft 2–3, 17, 20, 59, 115

de Certeau, Michel 17–18
de Cotret, Juli René 6, 66, 68, 73–5, 78
Deleuze, Gilles 5, 10, 12, 14–18, 20–3, 47–53, 77, 93–7, 114–15
dermis 7–8, 103–7, 109, 113–14
Derrida, Jacques 6, 25–9, 38, 46, 81, 93
desire 5, 38, 72, 86–9, 99–109, 114
Dickinson, Emily 57
dissonance 91, 97
domestic 2, 6, 37–8, 73
Douglas, Mary 6, 67–8, 71, 76–7
drape 23–4, 37, 65, 95, 97
dress 60–2, 65, 75–8
duPlessis, Rachel Blau 52–3
duplication 13, 41

ecstasy 102
edge 6–7, 36, 41, 43, 49–52, 58, 71, 81–2, 94–7, 107–14
ego 89
Eisenstein, Sergei 52–3
elastic 14, 16, 20, 33, 77
embellish 59–61
embroidery 16, 60–2
entangled 76, 91
erase 16–17, 85
erotic 54, 68, 82, 101, 103, 105–6
Ettinger, Bracha 3–4, 8, 10, 20
exorbitance 73, 102, 108–9
explicit 53, 63
exuberance 31, 37

felt 11, 15–17, 107–8
Fer, Briony 6, 31–5
fibre 31–2, 35, 51, 66, 72, 103
Flavin, Dan 33
fold 3–5, 11–24, 28, 95, 105, 111–15
fray 2, 4, 7, 21, 24, 71, 81–97, 111–14
Freud, Sigmund 7, 83, 86, 99–100

garment 13, 61, 73, 105
Gasché, Rodolphe 38
Gebauer and Wulf 93
gender 2, 7, 28
gestation 44, 49, 62
gesture 8, 27, 53, 62, 83, 88–92, 99–101, 105, 107–9
Gildart, Nancy 85
Guattari, Félix 10, 20, 93–4, 97, 114–15

Hamilton, Ann 6, 42, 44, 53–6
Haraway, Donna 81, 85, 90, 96
Harper, Catherine 42–3
Heidegger, Martin 13–14
Hemmings, Jessica 2, 32, 42–3
Hesse, Eva 6, 25–6, 31–8, 78, 117
Hicks, Sheila 21
hole 25–7, 35–6, 81, 84, 96
Holzer, Jenny 69–70, 72
hyphology 4, 69, 75, 78, 92

immanent 25, 77, 92
inflect 11, 14–15, 23, 115
interrelate 3, 22–3, 100
interstice 5, 24, 51–2, 61, 107
intertwine 1, 10, 23–4, 31, 47–9, 76, 95, 104, 106, 115
intimate 7–9, 16, 22, 32, 34, 37, 48, 54, 58, 61–5, 72, 86, 91, 100–8
Irigaray 8, 10, 13–15, 18, 42, 49–50, 57, 62, 67–70, 100–2, 104–9
Irmin, Rober 27

Jakobson, Roman 18–19
Jefferies, Janis 20–3, 41–3, 66, 71, 112–13
Johns, Jasper 33
Johnson, Pamela 9–10
jouissance 4

Klein, Melanie 9, 86–7
knitting 43, 106–7
knots 43, 108
Kristeva, Julia 30, 34, 48, 57, 67, 71–2, 76, 114
Kuder, Kristi Swee 7, 82, 90–2, 96

labour 6, 17, 60, 62, 85, 89, 91–2
labyrinth 5, 14–16, 22
Lacan, Jacques 43, 50
lace 26–8, 36, 76–7
Lackey, Jane 5, 15–23
lamination 47–9
Lawrence, Kay 70–2, 78
Lee, Pamela 32
Leibniz 5, 12, 23,
Levinas, Emmanuel 99, 101–3, 106
LeWitt, Sol 33–4
Lippard, Lucy 6, 31, 34, 36, 42
Livingstone, Joan 71, 85
logic 6, 11, 23, 26, 30, 32–7, 43, 74, 84, 93–4, 105, 108, 112
loom 2, 36, 91, 94, 114

MacCormack, Patricia 13–14, 18
machine 22, 44, 47–9
MacLeod, Kirsty 6, 42, 60–2
Maharaj, Sarat 20–4, 45–4, 112, 114
map 2, 11, 16–17, 22, 24, 53, 63, 85
Marks, Laura U. 8, 19, 55–6, 58–9, 69, 71, 74, 83, 89, 108
maternal 33, 48, 72
matrix 2–8, 14–16, 18–26, 36–8, 48, 57–8, 75–7, 109–15

matter 1–3, 6–7, 9, 17–20, 26, 32–9, 71–4
Medrez, Miriam 7, 82, 94–7
mend 83, 91, 94–5
Merleau-Ponty, Maurice 5, 10, 31, 104
metamorphosis 13, 15
metonymy 17–20, 43, 48
Metz, Stephanie 8, 100, 107–8
Middleton, Tricia 6, 26, 37–8
Millar, Lesley 26–8, 36, 77
Miller, Nancy 4, 84
Milner, Marion 74
mimesis 24, 42, 57–8, 60, 63, 74, 89, 92–4, 97, 108
Mitchell, Victoria 2–3, 41, 43–4
moiré 29, 91–2, 106
morphology 57, 68–9
mucous 67–72, 74, 77–9
muslin 66, 68

Naficy, Hamid 90
needle 6, 21, 41, 44–62, 70, 108
Neutral 6, 25–6, 29–33
Nietzsche, Friedrich 47
nomad 32, 58–9, 63, 90

organza 106

Pajaczkowska, Claire 2, 9, 41, 43, 75, 87–8, 91, 96
paradigm 15, 30–9, 51, 88
Parker, Rozsika 16–17
patch 6, 42–9, 59–60, 84–5, 96
Paterson, Mark 101–2
Pejic, Bojana 2
Perreault, Jeanne 42
phenomenology 5, 58, 100, 104, 114
pleasure 4, 29, 37, 71, 77–8, 104, 108
pleat 12–19, 21, 23

INDEX

pliable 16, 103
Polanyi, Michael 21–2
porous 7–8, 21–5, 37, 70, 82, 95–6, 100, 112–13
praxis 82, 87, 91
psychoanalysis 3, 5, 8–9, 86–9, 114, 118
psychology 8, 36, 48, 72

quilt 6, 42, 52, 59–60, 82–5, 96

realization 91
realized 71, 88
reflect 1, 3, 6, 9, 17, 25–39, 48–56, 62–3, 100, 111–12
reflexive 1, 12–13, 15, 20, 25, 39
represent 22–3, 37, 52, 55, 73, 89–90, 95, 117
rhetoric 84–5
rhizomatic 53
Robertson, Kirsty 2
Robinson, Hilary 57, 68–70
rupture 48–9, 55, 70–1, 90

Sartre, Jean-Paul 6, 66–8, 72–3, 75, 78, 99, 104
scar 51–4, 57, 63
schema 12, 16–17, 22, 51
Schneemann, Carolee 78
scintillates 10, 25–8, 31, 38
scissors l
scopic 37
screen 16–17, 23, 27, 39, 89, 117
scrim 16, 27, 117
seam 6, 19, 41–2, 44–53, 56–63, 92, 114
seaming 3–4, 6, 14, 24, 41–7, 49–55, 57–63, 111–14
seamstress 51, 61–2
secrete 11–12, 19, 22, 24, 29, 34, 36, 38–9, 44, 54–5, 67, 69–70, 72, 75–6, 78, 95, 107

selvedge 20, 82, 84–7, 92, 94
semiotic 26, 42, 48–9, 63
Sennett, Richard 26
sensation 38, 48, 72, 78, 102, 104, 107, 114
sensory 53, 55, 86
sensual 31, 67–8, 101
sew 42, 44, 48, 51, 57, 59
shimmer 3, 6, 24–39, 111, 113–14
Shiota, Chiharu 6, 66, 68–9, 75–8
Showalter, Elaine 3, 6, 41–2, 49, 52–3, 59–60, 82, 84, 96
silk 29, 45, 48, 54–5, 60–1, 65, 67–8, 106
Simon, Joan 21
skin 8, 33, 37, 48, 53, 67, 71–2, 100–4, 106–8, 114
Smith, T'ai 2, 41, 51, 61
Sobchack, Vivian 109
Sontag, Susan 19–21
Sorkin, Jenni 2, 9, 71
Spivak, Gyatri 7, 81–4, 90, 96
stain 9, 53, 71–2, 89
Stallybrass, Peter 44–5
Steihaug, Kari 8, 100, 105–6
Stewart, Susan 55–6
sticky 6–7, 13, 65–7, 71, 74–9, 113
stitch 1, 16–17, 19–20, 24, 43–52, 56–63, 66, 68–73, 78, 85
Studiowork 33–4, 117
surface 2–3, 6–11, 16–17, 23–9, 31–9, 50–9, 61, 67, 70–2, 74–9, 84, 95, 102–4, 107–14
suture 6, 44, 50–4, 56–7, 63

tacit 1, 7, 9, 21–2, 31, 53, 57, 63
tactic 8, 17, 42–3, 63, 82–3, 85, 96
tactile 21, 31, 55, 73, 100, 102, 104, 107

talith 28
techne 2–4, 43, 51
temporal 11–13, 15, 17, 21, 30, 50, 77, 94
textile-space 20–2, 115
thread 2, 6, 15, 20–9, 34–7, 41–50, 52–3, 57–62, 65–70, 72–8, 82, 88–96, 105–6, 111, 117
tissue 4, 9, 21, 51–2, 69, 75, 86, 89, 104
touch 13, 50, 79, 88–9, 99–105, 107–8, 113

Ullrich 29

Vasseleu, Cathryn 101–2
veil 6, 25, 27–9, 36–8, 45–6, 76, 90
velvet 114
Vervoordt 81–2, 97
Vidler 22–3
Virilio 11

viscous 4, 6–7, 24, 65–79, 111, 113–14
vision 27–9, 31–2, 38, 46, 50–2, 61, 67, 82, 86, 88, 90–1
voile 28

wadding 74
warp 2, 7–10, 15, 19, 28–31, 36, 38–9, 53, 58, 65–6, 81–4, 89–96, 100, 106–7, 113–15
weave 1–5, 7–10, 15–16, 20–9, 36, 53, 59, 65–8, 81–95, 100, 106–7, 114–15
weft 2, 7–10, 15, 19–21, 29, 31, 36, 53, 58, 65–6, 81–4, 89–96, 100, 106–7, 113–15
Whidden 6, 66, 68, 73–5, 78
Whitford 42, 57
Winnicott 9, 86–9
Wood Conroy 2, 27–8
Wyatt 6, 66, 68, 70–3, 78
Wyrwa 7, 82, 88